BROKEN YET CALLED

Paberback ISBN: 978-1-7370394-8-8
ePub ISBN: 978-1-7370394-9-5

Library of Congress Control Number (LCCN): 2022909244

Good Soil Press
St. Paul, Minnesota

Cover and interior design:
The Brand Office

BROKEN YET CALLED

A Leader's Journey to Renewal and Restoration

TERRANCE J. ROLLERSON

Good Soil Press

"My brother, friend, and Kingdom teammate, Terrance Rollerson, who I like to call "Pastor T," has written a book almost every pastor wants to write at some point in their ministry. It is a book about how churches and pastors are called to take care of each other, especially in times of brokenness. Terrance writes from his own experience, which is powerful, yet the book is practical for all. I find his writing to be balanced, thoroughly biblical, brutally honest, and blessedly practical. Pastors and church leaders, read this book together and respond as the Spirit leads. You will be grateful you did!"

—**DR. TIM ROEHL**, Author of *TransforMissional Coaching* and *Lead by Listening*, Blaine, Minnesota

"In *Broken Yet Called*, Reverend Terrance Rollerson has delivered a powerful admonishment to the Evangelical Christian community which has been infiltrated by cancel culture and hero worship. From the painful depths of his own brokenness, Rollerson has outlined a redemptive roadmap that local church bodies can prepare in advance to follow as they navigate brokenness, imperfection, and sins of their pastoral leadership. Churchgoers at every stage of engagement will gain a new perspective on Paul's words to the church in Galatia, 'Bear one another's burdens, and so fulfill the law of Christ.' (Galatians 6:2)"

—**JAMES WORDEN**, Deacon at Hope Community Church, Detroit, Michigan

"*Broken Yet Called* is a timely reminder of the importance of building the church and its relationships, both individual and corporate, around the personhood and mission of Christ! Pastor Rollerson, through lessons learned from his own journey, provides a roadmap for unity between congregations and pastors."

—**REVEREND JOSEPH HERD**, Grosse Pointe Woods, Michigan

"Broken Yet Called is a fresh and compelling invitation for the church to invest in renewing its leadership instead of just replacing it."

—**GREGORY DEMPSTER**, Founder and Director of ChristLife Ministries, Grand Rapids, Michigan

"Sadly, many churches and Christian organizations these days move to throw it/him/her away or ignore/deny/coverup the problem. These strategies are indicative of the broader culture for dealing with anyone who has made an error in judgment or behavior. Terrance Rollerson challenges pastors, congregations, and denominational ministerial overseers to seriously consider if there is a better way of reconciling and restoring a congregation, pastor, and others affected by a revelation of pastoral misconduct or brokenness. Out of his own painful experience, Pastor Terrance reminds us of the unique provisions we are given as the Body of Christ. He reminds us of the God-given promises, practices, and power we possess to partner with God as He seeks to bring about true and lasting healing and transformation. Our relationships are our primary witness to the world of God's great mercy and unsurpassable love!"

—**ANDREA ROLES**, M. Div., and Educator, St. Paul, Minnesota

"Rarely have I seen a book so masterfully identify a problem, engage with the scriptures regarding the solution to the problem, and provide a framework in which the church can implement the solutions outlined in the Bible. In this book, Pastor Terrance approaches the subject of church-leader brokenness not as a theoretician but as a practitioner, giving real life examples. I highly recommend this book to any church that is not only seeking to invite the Lord into the process of forgiveness, comfort, and reaffirmation of a broken church leader, ,but also for any church searching for ways to build a framework for better leader care."

—**REVEREND TED WILLIAMS**, Pastor, President of Banah Inn Caring Ministries, Crossville, Tennessee

"Pastor Terrance gently and graciously reminds us that we all come from a place of brokenness, including pastors and church leaders. *Broken Yet Called* will challenge and encourage you to see others how God sees them and to experience the freedom that comes from allowing God to work through our lives for His glory. As the church and the Body of Christ, may we be a place and a people offering healing and restoration to all those who need it."

—**TASHA NESS**, Board Trustee and Membership Partner at Urban Refuge Church, Minneapolis, Minnesota

"The church is a collection of broken attenders and broken leadership, and Terrance Rollerson has vividly captured a significant and critical issue facing the local church. His writing reflects the honesty and authenticity of his pain as well as his unrelenting faith in the One who heals. This book will guide many through their journey of brokenness."

—**DR. DONALD MORTENSON**, Associate Pastor at North Haven Church, Former Associate Professor at Bethel Theological Seminary, St. Paul, Minnesota

"In *Broken Yet Called*, Pastor T reminds us that God's forgiveness has no limits. Problems fracture people and relationships, but God leads us to the solution. He loves the church and wants to see broken people and broken systems within the church experience restoration. *Broken Yet Called* provides a roadmap for God's people to experience the fullness of restoration with no limits. Enjoy this treasure!

—**REVEREND LEON R. STEVENSON III**, Pastor, Mack Avenue Community Church, Detroit, Michigan

This book is dedicated
to my dear wife, Michelle.

She is the love of my life, and without her support,
I could not have written this book.
She encouraged me through seminary,
becoming a pastor, planting a church,
and pastoring five other churches.
Michelle stood with me in my brokenness
and prayed over me as we sought God's direction
in our lives. I am so very thankful for her.
To God be the glory!

TABLE OF CONTENTS

FOREWORD

In December of 1996, American movie goers were drawn to the box office to view a new comedy holiday release by Touchstone Pictures entitled *The Preacher's Wife*, adapted from the 1947 film, *The Bishop's Wife* by Leonardo Bercovici and Robert E. Sherwood, which came from a novel by Robert Nathan. *The Preacher's Wife* touted an all-star cast, including, Denzel Washington, Courtney B. Vance, Loretta Devine, and the extraordinary songstress, Whitney Houston. The storyline of the movie follows Reverend Henry Biggs, who pastors a small, struggling African American Baptist Church in New York City. Reverend Biggs is facing a plethora of problems, including financial challenges, declining membership, an aging building, and a bad case of self-doubt about his ability to lead. To make matters worse, Reverend Biggs has sorely neglected his wife and son, who feel his frustration and bear the brunt of his stress and worry. A desperate prayer sent up to heaven is answered through the visitation of an angel named

Dudley, who arrives on the scene in an attempt to get Reverend Biggs to understand what matters in life and in ministry—love and hope.

Of course, we know that angels do not manifest themselves as Dudley in this iconic movie, but what we can relate to are the challenges experienced by Reverend Biggs. Many of us have our own Reverend Biggs serving our congregations. There is nothing easy about being a pastor. Understanding how to adequately care for a flock, praying through, preparing for, and delivering sermons week after week, addressing individual and familial concerns of church members, officiating weddings and funerals, and attending to the broader affairs of the church and the like can all wreak havoc on the personal and professional life of clergy. There is, of course, great beauty and meaning in the call to minister to a flock, but the reality, as research shows, is that many pastors are struggling to maintain mental, emotional, and familial health. Many are burning out or are leaving the profession altogether. Churches need to understand the very real challenges that clergy face, to humanize their pain and frustrations, and to refrain from idolizing the role or the person. In short, pastors need our support.

Reverend Terrence Rollerson's book, *Broken Yet Called*, is an honest and forthright examination of the challenges that both he and other pastors have faced. Whether it be exhaustion, depression, emotional brokenness, or dishonesty of some kind, the call of the book is to normalize the need for both self-reflection and organizational support for clergy and their church members. At the end of each chapter, adequate space has been provided to write down revelations that come as a result of individual or small group reading. The hope is that each of us will become clearer on how we can both support and uplift our pastors and church leaders in their journey to vocational wholeness and optimal health.

My relationship with Pastor Rollerson has spanned more than twenty-five years. I know personally his love for his wife, Michelle, their children, and the Church. I have prayed with, cried with, and served alongside this dear brother who has selflessly given his life to raise up godly disciples who will remain steadfast and committed Christ-followers for a lifetime. My prayer for all who read this book is that you will gain new insights into how to come alongside your pastors in healthy times as well as in hard times, and to treat them with love and grace as they are called to wholeness and holiness.

—REVEREND LAUREL M. BUNKER, St. Paul, Minnesota

INVITATION

One of my favorite invitations given to us by our mighty God is to "taste and see that the Lord is good" (Psalm 34:8). As we walk through this world, we can sometimes lose our way. We begin to drift from God's hope for us as we become distracted with the things we watch, listen to, put up with, or do. But at every turn, God is there with us in the midst of our mess. He stands ready to renew us from the inside out.

While the words on the following pages are directed toward pastors and churches, I believe anyone will be able to engage in this journey. If you have past wounds that continue to inform your present, I want you to know there is hope! It is a hope that is deeply rooted in the love that is given to us by our living God, through the death and resurrection of Jesus Christ, and sealed with the power of the Holy Spirit.

I have watched God move in the lives of people in some powerful ways over the last twenty years, but I must admit that I was somewhat caught off guard when I was confronted with an area of my own brokenness. There has been no other time in my life where I have felt more lost and alone. As I went through this difficult, painful, and confusing time, which I will explain further as we go along, I continued to claim my hope in God as the one who deeply desires for us to live out who He has created us to be. Part of His desire is that what has been broken and distorted will be redeemed and made beautiful. If we are willing to see and confront our brokenness or walk beside someone else confronting their brokenness, then newness, redemption, and restoration will be found! It will take time and requires surrendering of the things we hold onto. I make this bold statement because I have experienced it myself. Praise God for the redeeming grace available to us!

"Amazing Grace"
Words by John Newton, 1779

Amazing grace, how sweet the sound
That saved a wretch like me
I once was lost, but now am found
T'was blind but now I see

T'was grace that taught my heart to fear
And grace, my fears relieved
How precious did that grace appear
The hour I first believed

Through many dangers, toils and snares
We have already come.
T'was grace that brought us safe thus far
And grace will lead us home,
And grace will lead us home

Amazing grace, how sweet the sound
That saved a wretch like me
I once was lost but now am found
T'was blind but now I see
Was blind, but now I see.[1]

What is the meaning behind this grace that is so amazing? Merriram-Webster.com defines grace as, "a: unmerited divine assistance given to humans for their regeneration or sanctification, b: a virtue coming from God, c: a state of sanctification enjoyed through divine assistance." [2]

"Amazing Grace" is a clear reminder that we have been redeemed and restored by God's grace and mercy. It is God's gift of grace that has allowed me to discover a new and bold vision of grace and love for churches and the people who serve them. God's amazing grace has set me right with an amazing God who loves me, even with my flaws, and works to move me to a place of wholeness. This amazing grace not only places me in the eternal care of a loving God, but it also delivers me from my brokenness.

When our faith communities extend grace and have a plan for restoration, healing is made possible. It takes both risk and effort to journey through the difficult work, and each time, I believe we grow a little more into the likeness of Christ. Having an area of brokenness is nothing less than bondage in a specific area of life, which we all experience. Grace, by way of the death and resurrection of Jesus Christ, delivers us to freedom! Whenever and wherever His grace shows up, it is a sweet melody that carries us to freedom.

I believe we see the glory of God at work in the moments that are the hardest for us to extend grace. A spouse forgiving a spouse, a parent expressing love toward a wayward child, a survivor forgiving the violator, and yes, a church staying in the fight with a pastor whose brokenness has come to the attention of the faith community, are all examples of God working through His people to extend grace when it is needed most.

Many people walk through this life wondering how they can see or be part of the glory of God. His glory is on full display when those of us who are followers of Jesus extend the grace that has been extended to us. It is in these moments that we get a greater glimpse of the glory of God.

Grace is much more than unmerited favor. It is the power of God at work within us and among us to bring God's desired transformation to our individual lives and to our life together. Grace brings forth power and light. A.W. Tozer said in his book, *The Knowledge of the Holy*, "Grace is the good pleasure of God that inclines Him to bestow benefits on the undeserving."[3] John MacArthur goes a step further in *The Truth About Grace* and says, "Grace is not merely unmerited favor; it is favor bestowed on sinners who deserve death."[4]

Showing kindness to a stranger is unmerited favor but doing good to one's enemies is made possible only by the empowerment of the Holy Spirit. Grace is about relationships being untethered to conditions or personal perspectives. It is not about them; it is about us! It is God and me, God and you, and God and us. It is the Holy Spirit let loose in our lives and in our relationships. What a privilege!

CHAPTER ONE

THE QUESTION

Before we dive in too deep, let's process the most important question(s) together. Can a pastor have brokenness in an area of his or her life and still be effective within the context of pastoring? Since we are all sinners, there is some common ground on which we can all agree. Pastors are imperfect, just like everyone else, yet they are called to be the leader of their congregation. The point of disagreement on this issue comes when we try to define "how much brokenness" or "which kind of brokenness" we are willing to accept in our pastors. Under what kind of circumstances is it appropriate, in fact, faithful, for the church to commit to a process of extending grace to the pastor? As people of God, *how* is this determined or discerned, and *how* does the Body of Christ and the pastor proceed to live this out? It becomes difficult to process when disagreements surface, so we must turn to what God's Word has to say about it.

If the pastor has been confronted biblically, recognized the sin, and asked for forgiveness, the pastor is in a posture of humility and stands ready to do the work necessary to move toward healing and wholeness. It must be a Holy Spirit-driven process! There will be people within the church body who cannot or will not forgive the pastor no matter what. That is a subject for another time or perhaps another book. I am not talking about a few people in the church; I am talking about the church body actively participating in extending grace. This is something we aren't always accustomed to doing for our church leaders.

Our greatest desire as pastors is that the church we serve would be a beacon of light to the people in its community who are wounded, weary, lost, and broken. We hope that through both the grace of God and the work of God, the community of *people* in and outside of the sanctuary would not *at all* be surprised by the messiness of people's lives and willingly stand with them before a loving God.

Our churches are places of safety and love, but can pastors be included in the body of believers, or do they linger just outside the gates? I don't hear others asking this question, but we must admit that the answer gets at our fundamental belief of the roles we play in serving one another, pastor and congregation, in order to advance the Kingdom of God. I hear you. It is not lost on me that there are situations where the Body of Christ may have to let a pastor go because of the level of brokenness operating in the pastor's life. I'm not here to present a list of brokenness that a church should consider forgivable. I simply want to journey with you through this as we wrestle with it on all sides, both from the perspective of the pastor and from the perspective of the church.

There are blessings to be received both individually and corporately in the complexities that come while extending grace. As churches and pastors lean into their vision and lay a solid foundation of grace, I hope we can resist our cultural throw-away or cancel mindset long enough to really consider what God would have us do.

As churches and pastors lean into their vision and lay a solid foundation of grace, I hope we can resist our cultural throw-away or cancel mindset long enough to really consider what God would have us do.

God's divine restoration plan is like no other. He calls for churches and pastors to live out His promise of provision and restoration. God wants—in fact, *longs*—to provide grace for the toughest of situations, but He doesn't force it upon us. We need to put on our God-sized lens so we can see situations in need of grace and restoration.

I now more fully realize that we must stand on the power God gives to restore. We are to be a reflection of Christ, even in the most difficult moments. These are the moments where we can choose to be better or to be bitter. We can walk around in freedom or with a chip on our shoulder. We have been redeemed by the blood of the Lamb; it came at a great cost and with great difficulty. We often forget about this great sacrifice and the power that is available to us if we only ask for it.

Where brokenness is met with forgiveness, renewal, restoration, and reinstatement, there will be much prayer, discernment, and trust in a God who is not surprised by the variety of strong emotions that a church experiences amid the brokenness and restoration process. Through it all, however, we are invited by God to "taste and see that the Lord is good" (Psalm 34:8).

God is especially good at helping us handle the chaos that ensues in the wake of brokenness. We must not forget the second half of the previous verse: "Blessed is the man who takes refuge in Him!" The Church has for far too long said, "Let's just get all of this behind us as soon as we can." This mindset can do far more harm than good in the church's quest to be a beacon in their community and to help the members of their congregation grow in faith and love.

The world teaches us how to push through, sweep under the carpet, forget, cancel, and get on with it! What the world does not show us is how to stick with and stay with someone in the middle of hard times. That is much harder.

When a church does not allow people to safely and appropriately express and process the varied emotions that come because of a pastor's brokenness, an unhealthy pattern begins. Moving to another church or retiring might seem easier at the time, but the emotions go "underground" and potentially create hidden agendas or too much power among different people in the church. We are called to minister to one another, to do hard things, helping both the individuals and the congregation come through the experience of loss, healthy and ready for the future God has planned.

We tend to have a limited vision of grace when the brokenness goes beyond the limits we set by our own experience and understanding. Grace is often granted with the thought that "they better not mess up again." This is not at all the framework of God's grace. It is the seventy-seven-times-seven process that God spells out for us in the Bible.

The Jewish rabbis of Jesus' day taught that you only had to extend forgiveness three times. So, in Matthew 18:21-22, when Peter asked the question, "Lord, how many times shall I forgive my sister or brother who sins against me?" Peter had in mind what he had been taught and likely felt he was being generous to forgive seven times. But in God's forgiveness system, forgiveness has no limits.

This does not mean the person sinning can skip repenting and go on sinning. Repentance is a must, but it's only one side of the equation! God is saying that for the person extending the forgiveness, there should be no limit to the number of times they forgive.

If we read on just a few more verses, we find that Jesus uses the parable of a king wanting to settle the accounts of his servants. The servant that had his debt forgiven would not forgive the debt of his fellow servant. Matthew 18:32-33 says, "Then his master summoned him and said to him, 'You wicked servant! I forgave you all that debt

The world teaches us how to push through, sweep under the carpet, forget, cancel, and get on with it! What the world does not show us is how to stick with and stay with someone in the middle of hard times. That is much harder.

because you pleaded with me. And should not you have had mercy on your fellow servant, as I had mercy on you?'"

What encouragement this is for all of us! God has extended great grace and tender mercy on each of us. It is out of that gift that we extend it to others. It is even in the famous Lord's Prayer, "and forgive us our debts (sin), as we also have forgiven our debtors" (Matthew 6:12).

I invite us to hear this very clearly: God perfectly forgives, and He does it all the time. This is our model to strive after. Humanly, this is not always easy to do. But as we give what was divinely given to us, we display the glory of God working in us and through us.

REFLECTIONS ON THE JOURNEY

As a way to enter into a conversation with God about restoration, take some time to give thanks and rejoice in God's character and promise, turning to Him in faith and in love. Read the verse below and develop a Prayer, Petition, and Praise based on the chapter and verse.

Exodus 34:6-7

"The Lord passed before him and proclaimed, The Lord, the Lord, a God merciful and gracious, slow to anger, and abounding in steadfast love and faithfulness, keeping steadfast love for thousands, forgiving iniquity and transgression and sin, but who will by no means clear the guilty, visiting the iniquity of the fathers on the children and the children's children, to the third and the fourth generation."

Prayer (confession and listening) _____

_____

_____

_____

Petition (our needs) _____

_____

_____

_____

Praise (bringing Him glory) _____

_____

_____

_____

_____

CHAPTER TWO

THE CASE FOR GRACE

Case Study #1: David

David was a hero—an anointed King—and Jesus came through his family line. David was a talented musician and a songwriter. His gentleness as a harpist was telling of his sensitive spirit, his music the only thing that seemed to sooth King Saul when he would feel dark spirits surrounding him. David tended the royal family's sheep, and his defeat of Goliath is one of the most famous stories in the Bible. Scripture declares that David was a man after God's heart.

As a centerpiece of the Book of Psalms, we have the depth of David's pursuit of God as expressed in Psalm 63:1-3: "O God, you are my God; earnestly I seek you; my soul thirsts for you; my flesh faints for you, as in a dry and weary land where there is no water. So I have looked upon you in the sanctuary, beholding your power and glory. Because your steadfast love is better than life, my lips will praise you."

If there is a case to be made for an Old Testament figure who is a model for following after God, David would be one, yet we also see in David a man who truly blew it! When the kings were off to war, King David made a *very* poor decision. It wasn't his usual practice. Bad judgment on King David's part set the stage for his devastating fall into sin. As it reads in 2 Samuel 11:1-5, "In the spring of the year, the time when kings go out to battle, David sent Joab, and his servants with him, and all Israel. And they ravaged the Ammonites and besieged Rabbah. But David remained at Jerusalem. It happened, late one afternoon, when David arose from his couch and was walking on the roof of the king's house, that he saw from the roof a woman bathing; and the woman was very beautiful. And David sent and inquired about the woman. And one said, 'Is not this Bathsheba, the daughter of Eliam, the wife of Uriah the Hittite?' So David sent messengers and took her, and she came to him, and he lay with her. (Now she had been purifying herself from her uncleanness.) Then she returned to her house. And the woman conceived, and she sent and told David, 'I am pregnant.'"

King David plotted successfully to have Bathsheba's husband killed in battle so he could take her as his wife. In a single bad decision, David displayed adultery, deception, conspiracy, murder, and lying. David's action was so bad that his best friend, Nathan, confronted David with his sin in such a way that the king would clearly see that his actions were a sin against God.

We see in Psalm 51:1-9 that David pleads for forgiveness; he confesses and owns his sin. He cries out for God to restore his joy and not take the Holy Spirit from him. It is important to note that the Holy Spirit did not dwell in people in the way the Holy Spirit dwells in people today. When David asks not to have the Spirit taken from him, he is literally asking that God would not remove His presence.

In 2 Samuel, chapter 12, we see how Nathan's rebuke and David's confession and restoration played out. This is the part of the Bible

THE CASE FOR GRACE

story that ordinarily gets less attention. As we consider this chapter and how David was restored, we should stand in amazement of the mercy and grace of the Lord in providing for the atonement (covering) of our sins. God's mercy triumphs over judgment when a humbled, repentant sinner turns back to the Lord. Conviction leads to recognition of sin, which leads to confession, which is a step toward accountability, restoration, and eventually, transformation. What a beautiful opportunity before us to help others through this miraculous process!

Let's be honest. There are indeed certain moments, especially when sinners deny their sin, that require rebuke. While David certainly experienced real-life consequences of his sin, God not only restored him to a relationship with himself, but He also continued to bless David as the King of Israel. This is the character of our God and the model by which we should seek to live out our lives with one another.

There is no doubt that David had great responsibility and many difficult times. The Book of Psalms seems to indicate that David spent a great deal of time before the Lord pleading for God's presence to remain with him. God did not leave David alone but filled him in ways that enabled him to fulfill his call.

Case Study #2: Paul
While David seemed to have God's hand on him from the time of his youth, Paul, also known as Saul of Tarsus, was impacted by God later in life. Paul was a Hebrew among Hebrews. He had a Jewish heritage, discipline, and zeal that could not be matched. Paul was a Roman citizen, which gave him rights that others did not have.

We know from the Bible that Paul started at least twelve churches. His missionary journeys took him throughout the Roman empire, and he authored thirteen books of the Bible. Many would say he was the biggest champion for Christianity to ever live.

In Philippians 3:4-6, Paul says that if anyone should be saved by their religiosity, it should be him: "Though I myself have reason for confidence in the flesh also. If anyone else thinks he has reason for confidence in the flesh, I have more: circumcised on the eighth day, of the people of Israel, of the tribe of Benjamin, a Hebrew of Hebrews; as to the law, a Pharisee; as to zeal, a persecutor of the church; as to righteousness under the law, blameless."

We know that Paul was a formidable person committed to his Jewishness. We also know that he was a mighty man, doing good work on behalf of the Kingdom of God. There was a shift that took place for Paul on the road to Damascus—on the way to fulfill his licensed work to kill Christians. We can be thankful that God stepped in, giving Paul an entirely new framework for seeing himself. He went from Saul, the Jewish Pharisee, to Paul, the Christian church planter!

Listen to what is said in 1 Timothy 1:12-17: "I thank him who has given me strength, Christ Jesus our Lord, because he judged me faithful, appointing me to his service, though formerly I was a blasphemer, persecutor, and insolent opponent. But I received mercy because I had acted ignorantly in unbelief, and the grace of our Lord overflowed for me with the faith and love that are in Christ Jesus. The saying is trustworthy and deserving of full acceptance, that Christ Jesus came into the world to save sinners, of whom I am the foremost. I received mercy for this reason, that in me, as the foremost, Jesus Christ might display his perfect patience as an example to those who were to believe in him for eternal life. To the King of the ages, immortal, invisible, the only God, be honor and glory forever and ever."

Paul clearly recognized his brokenness and the grace that was given to him. He saw himself as the worst kind of sinner, yet the goodness of God prevailed in Paul's life, moving him from darkness to light, death to life, destitute to eternal life. Paul reminds us in verse 15 that Jesus came into this world to save sinners like you and like me.

Throughout Paul's letters, it's clear to see that he has a deep understanding of God's grace. It is completely undeserved, and because it is such a priceless gift, it compels a loving response from those who receive it. "To me, though I am the very least of all the saints, this grace was given, to preach to the Gentiles the unsearchable riches of Christ" (Ephesians 3:8).

God's grace took a terrorist toward Christ followers, saved him, renewed him, and used him for the glory of His Kingdom. This is the God we serve! He finds us in some of our darkest moments and brings us into His light. God is never done with us no matter how wrong we go. When we turn toward Him, hear His voice, and follow Him, we are always found by Him.

There is an entire list of people in the Bible who display God's heart toward humanity, Moses, Peter, Paul, Noah, and David to name a few. It is a heart that desires to put people back into right fellowship with God—that His glory would be seen, and His Gospel would be spoken in order for our hearts and lives to be transformed.

God *is* love and therefore, God will never cease to extend His love, always hoping to see those who He created in His image turn to Him for loving relationship. God will never consider any of us too far gone to be reached by His love! Our value is never a question for God. Our actions may need to be questioned but never our value. God is in the renewal and restoration business. As we seek to join Him in this work, all praise, glory, and honor belong to God.

REFLECTIONS ON THE JOURNEY

As a way to enter into a conversation with God about restoration, take some time to give thanks and rejoice in God's character and promise, turning to Him in faith and in love. Read the verse below and develop a Prayer, Petition, and Praise based on the chapter and verse.

2 Corinthians 12:9

"But he said to me, "My grace is sufficient for you, for my power is made perfect in weakness." Therefore I will boast all the more gladly of my weaknesses, so that the power of Christ may rest upon me."

Prayer (confession and listening) _____

_____

_____

_____

Petition (our needs) _____

_____

_____

_____

Praise (bringing Him glory) _____

_____

_____

_____

CHAPTER THREE

BROKENNESS

I have been blessed to be involved in the lives of a few thousand people. With each church that I have had the great pleasure to pastor, I have felt loved. I am so thankful for each of those churches and the loving people who attend and work there. They helped me grow in ways too numerous to count.

My fifth church was special. I was in my mid-50s, and after being a solo pastor, a lead pastor with an assistant, a youth director, a church planter, and a co-pastor with two other pastors, I was blessed to be asked to be the senior pastor of a church that had several full-time staff, great church leadership, and an active prayer team, all unified in their mission and fully supportive of one another. At this point in my journey of pastoring, this church was an ideal fit and quite possibly the last church I would serve before retirement.

The brokenness I experienced began to show itself just months after starting my dream job and came in an unexpected way. As a pastor, an essential part of one's job and ministry is preparing a sermon each week. I was blessed to be a part of a preaching team so I would not be preparing over fifty sermons a year. I loved that I could share this part of my ministry so the church body could hear different, trusted voices from the pulpit. I also knew there would be a natural spotlight on me, the new senior pastor, and it was important for me to deliver good messages. After several months had gone by, I began to hear criticism from some that my sermons were not meeting their needs or expectations.

This impacted me deeply for several reasons, some of which I have come to better understand in the last few months and years. When I encounter criticism, my inner voice starts to speak loudly, saying, *I am not good enough.* Any of you have a voice like that? It can be a bit overwhelming. When the criticism began to surface, my inner voice worked to convince me that I was unable to formulate words that stimulate and stir the souls of the people I had been given to feed. I desperately wanted to be that pastor whose words put a stamp on the hearts of the people I was called to pastor. I wanted to succeed. To hear that I was not doing that for all people meant I was failing, I decided. You see, my speaking abilities are at the heart of how I am judged as a pastor, yet, that very skill, and my confidence surrounding it, is threatened by a disability. I have dyslexia. It's been a lifelong struggle, though it was not officially diagnosed until my second year of college after being put on academic probation three times. I spent my entire childhood and teenage years feeling that I did not have what it took to be academically or professionally successful. For many years prior to diagnosis, I thought I was just dumb and spent all my effort trying to cover up my inadequacies.

Although I was not consciously aware of this at the time, when I find myself backed into a corner by criticism or failure, I defend myself by trying to perform my way out. I was just a few months into serving this church and understandably anxious to establish myself and demonstrate who I was as the new senior pastor. I knew my sermons had to be exceptional in order to appease those who were grumbling.

As I came across sermon ideas, I started using the words of other pastors and not giving them proper credit. As I continued to feel enormous pressure to produce quality sermons, I held privately my dyslexia and fears of not being good enough. I am sad to say that I plagiarized part or all of sermons of other pastors and delivered them as my own. This was clearly wrong. My dyslexia was not and is not a proper excuse, and it was a very bad decision.

Naturally, it was eventually discovered and reported to the leadership of the church that I was using words that were not my own. Dreadfully, I was confronted. The church leadership granted me grace and mercy, and as a leadership team, we talked about the importance of this being a line that should not be crossed again.

This should have been the end of the story.

But I am sad to admit that I failed again.

And I failed more than once.

I had agreed that this was a line that should not be crossed, and that I would work to use my own words in my messages going forward. While not an excuse for any of this being right in any circumstance, it seems important that I give you a little background on what was going on during the time I plagiarized those sermons. Church attendance and giving were down (felt responsible), my vision for the church was not received well by some members of the congregation (felt rejected), some thought I did not understand the ethos of the church (felt mistrusted), and some said I wanted to change the church (felt misunderstood).

The emotions I was feeling were not wrong, it's that I let them take over my mind. I did not reflect on what was truly going on.

All these voices were like a neon light flashing, "Rejected. Rejected. Rejected. You are not good enough. You are all alone. You have to figure this out."

At the time, I didn't really understand where all these emotions were coming from, but through prayer and counseling, I came to recognize that feeling abandoned as a child by both my parents made me hypersensitive toward rejection or feeling unloved. My deep-seeded belief that I was never good enough, combined with the very real limitations brought on by my dyslexia, made the conditions ripe for failure. I found myself in an emotional tailspin that I could not stop. Even though I made a genuine agreement with church leadership to stop using the words of others, I was so beyond repair emotionally that I could not even recognize that I was breaking their trust again.

I hit rock bottom.

I fully own my failure. There was some significant brokenness in me surrounding my growing-up years and my dyslexia that needed to be addressed and healed. You see, I grew up in the foster care system in the Bronx throughout my adolescence and into my teen years. I desperately desired to be loved. Unfortunately, I did not receive the love I needed from my foster parents. I did not know my biological father, and I met my biological mother just once. Understandably so, I was suspicious of whether or not she loved me. But when I came into a relationship with Jesus Christ, I heard Him say, "I will love you forever!" At the time, I simply did not understand the depth of my brokenness and how it was affecting me.

Have you ever been in a similar place?

Do you know someone who is?

The result of my personal brokenness and failure meant the church was in turmoil. My actions hurt many people. They were left feeling betrayed because I had broken the trust they had placed in me. Because of my poor choices, I had not lived up to who I should have been *or* wanted to be as a senior pastor.

The church leadership still felt there was a path forward that would lead to restoration, some church members felt my actions should cost me my job, and other church members felt my actions could be forgiven and I could retain my job after a time of counseling and healing. The various strongly held views of how to move forward threatened to split the congregation.

I had never experienced being in the center of a church where a number of people wanted to see me out the door. We've all heard of pastors going through a variety of situations that resulted in their immediate dismissal. There are no words that can speak to the emotions I felt when I learned that people wanted to leave the church because of *me*. It was a very agonizing time for my wife and me.

The turmoil about my sermon plagiarism turned into sectors of our church living in disagreement. This resulted in more wounds, not just for me, but also for the church as a whole. I could not bear seeing the church stuck on this controversial issue, regardless of the church leadership's vision for restoration and my commitment to change.

I chose to resign.

My wife, Michelle, and I felt God would honor our choice, and that with that choice, the church would rediscover unity and recommit to their God-given identity and mission. With this decision, I found myself in uncharted waters. This place of uncertainty and inner turmoil was not familiar to me. To be bluntly honest, I was wrecked on so many levels. I missed the people. I missed the sense of community. I missed serving. I missed stepping into what God had for us to do. I felt lost and alone. I felt broken and helpless, and for a while, I did not know which way to turn. If truth be told, I didn't even know if I deserved to have grace extended to me. *How could God forgive me?*

Do I even deserve to be forgiven? These were my questions, and the perceived answers were *No.*

I was aware that it would take a mighty work of God to move me from my solemn state. I desperately needed to see a glimmer of His goodness. That was when I committed to the task of honestly and biblically taking a long look at myself. It would not (and did not) happen overnight. I had to do some real soul searching. I needed to take an introspective look at what had led me to a place where I never chose to be. I knew deep down it was not really about sermon preparation or even my dyslexia.

I told the story of my failure over and over to a wide variety of people, and of all the people I needed to tell my story to, the most difficult people were my immediate and extended family. It was so very difficult to tell my young adult children who had seen me serve in churches their entire lives. They had never seen me go through such pain. Watching their dad work through this was a real-life education, and my hope was that they saw me journey toward restoration with dignity and honor. I am extremely thankful for their support.

After taking time to soul search, with the help of some grace- and Spirit-filled people, I gained a greater understanding of how my past was still influencing me. I had always held to the belief that it's best to just leave the past behind. To some extent, that attitude had served me well. I never saw myself as a victim, just an overcomer.

The attitude of an overcomer was how a boy who grew up in the projects on the south side of the Bronx was able to get a college degree, a master's degree, and become a pastor. Not allowing my past to hold me back had indeed served me well, but I would not recommend it as a lifelong habit. For me, it came at a cost and that bill came due.

God graciously keeps inviting us to these places of acknowledgement and healing over time, have you noticed? Unfortunately, we often fail to pay attention to His nudging because we're afraid it will be painful or require too much work or patience. Many times, after we come to know Christ, we hold some areas back, believing that the God who created the heavens and the earth, lit the stars, and hung the sun and the moon, will not notice that we are hiding things from Him. This can be both conscious and subconscious, but nevertheless, there are some things in our lives that go unsurrendered to our Lord. The yuck we *think* we hide from God, that's the yuck He wants to *free* us from! The God we serve wants all of us, even the ugly stuff that we try to hide.

It is important to understand that the pastor and the church can partner with the work of the Holy Spirit to bring restoration and freedom to everyone. I am here to challenge pastors and churches to live out the model of God's character, rich with grace, mercy, and love.

Once I got to the place in my personal crisis where the fog started to lift, I began to wonder if churches could be more prepared to stand with their pastor when brokenness comes. I believe God is calling us to do more. I was able to find restoration and healing, but not everyone has the support and the freedom of time to do so. Many are dealing with long-term damage for how they were treated and/or fired. If this is you, or if you know of someone who is feeling wounded, please let this be an encouragement to them and to you, my brothers and sisters. Together, we can find a better way to bring restoration and healing to our churches where there is division, misunderstanding, brokenness, and pain. To God be the glory!

Many times, after we come to know Christ, we hold some areas back, believing that the God who created the heavens and the earth, lit the stars, and hung the sun and the moon, will not notice that we are hiding things from Him.

REFLECTIONS ON THE JOURNEY

As a way to enter into a conversation with God about restoration, take some time to give thanks and rejoice in God's character and promise, turning to Him in faith and in love. Read the verse below and develop a Prayer, Petition, and Praise based on the chapter and verse.

Isaiah 41:10

"Fear not, for I am with you; be not dismayed, for I am your God; I will strengthen you, I will help you, I will uphold you with my righteous right hand."

Prayer (confession and listening) _____

_____

_____

_____

Petition (our needs) _____

_____

_____

_____

Praise (bringing Him glory) _____

_____

_____

_____

CHAPTER FOUR

THE QUEST

So now that we've established a need for churches to be better equipped for these situations when they arise, is there a biblical case for how and why a church can and should work with a pastor in an area of brokenness? This is a critical question, and please know that there is no easy answer. We don't want to make a pastor feel ashamed nor do we want to call out the church for being unforgiving. There are even situations where a pastor must leave, yet the home church could play a more central role in the healing process. No matter the scenario, my hope is that we consider an alternative solution where space is given to pastors as churches participate in the journey toward grace that Christ has extended to all of us.

Somehow along the way, evangelical Christian churches have allowed their compass to move a little off true North. "God shows His love for us in that while we were still sinners, Christ died for us" (Romans 5:8). We must remember that we were not found by Christ perfected, but we were found in the midst of our mess.

I have been on a journey ever since that day I submitted my resignation. There are a number of areas where I have been set free from bondage. All praise and honor belong to the Lord! However, there are other areas that have proven to be a longer journey. I am so thankful that God doesn't give up on drawing us closer to Himself, and that He continues to grow us into His image.

Paul tells us in Romans 7:15 that there is an ongoing battle within each of us: "For I do not understand my own actions. For 'I do not do what I want, but I do the very thing that I hate.'" When we recognize we are in this kind of battle, we are hard pressed to find victories unless we step into the full view, seeing who we are and whose we are through the lens of the death and resurrection of Jesus Christ.

In so doing, I have discovered a better understanding for myself by way of Romans 12:2: "Do not be conformed to this world, but be transformed by the renewal of your mind, that by testing you may discern what is the will of God, what is good and acceptable and perfect."

I don't know about you, but for years, my eyes and my actions have been on being transformed by the renewal of my mind. This is not a bad or a wrong notion, but I had not considered the very part of this verse that calls me not to be conformed to this world.

You're familiar with my story now, but there is an important part of my personal discovery that I haven't mentioned yet. As a person who lives with dyslexia, I have worked hard not to allow it to be a crutch for what I cannot do. I would speak those words out loud in many settings. But the truth is, I had, and still have sometimes, a deep-seated belief that I am not enough as it pertains to learning or being what people expect me to be as a pastor. I have come to understand that I had been viewing my dyslexia from a "conforming to the world" point of view. I was measuring myself by what I thought the world expected of me.

When I heard God's call for me to be a pastor, I heard it in a particular way. I believe God wanted to use my life experiences to touch the lives of others. I did not consider, however, that my dyslexia could be an integral part of my calling. Much to the contrary. I believed that my dyslexia was a broken, shameful part of me and thought God was calling me *in spite* of my dyslexia. For years, I allowed myself to be backed into corners where I would have to navigate or perform my way out.

Do you see the problem? How do I live life as a pastor worth anything if I have serious doubts about my own abilities? So, when critical voices caused my self-doubt to flare up, my own negative self-talk began to get louder and overshadow how God views me. The truth for me is that God was and is fully aware of my dyslexia, and it is actually *part* of His calling for me. God wants to use all of us, our shortcomings included!

I wonder if churches today see the broken parts of a pastor as part of the journey for what God is doing with them. . .*together*? My experience tells me that most do not see it this way. Both the pastor and the church have much to gain through a shared moment of brokenness and the healing that follows.

Pastors are not perfected humans sent to a church to stand as the model of what it looks like to be fully invested in Christ's plan. Pastors are people with varying levels of brokenness—just like everyone else who is on staff or attends that church. Our greatest opportunity in helping people grow is to provide a safe space for brokenness to be acknowledged and prayerfully brought before God with the encouraging, faithful, wise, and discerning support of our brothers and sisters in Christ. There is apprehension to do this because in our culture today, pastors are placed on a self-imposed or a church-imposed pedestal.

My challenge to those who have received the call to be a pastor is to live out of the gifts that have been given to them. We need to stop trying to add to that gifting based on what or how others think we should be gifted. And we should not overlook the broken pieces because they may be just the gift that God is calling us to use. In the hands of the Redeemer, these areas can become the anointing oil that soothes the aches of others. My dyslexia in the hands of the Redeemer has enabled me to have compassion, patience, and insight with others who are dealing with areas that hinder their work or cause them to believe a lie about their abilities.

My quest is to help churches and pastors see each other from a biblical point of view, to stop seeing themselves as two separate parts but instead, as one body. God uses the health of a pastor to help the church and the health of a church to help the pastor. In caring for a pastor in the midst of brokenness, God is caring for the church as well. We are all part of one body, the Body of Christ.

Pastors are not hired hands being brought in simply to "do a job," and churches are not an employer simply seeking "the best talent" they can afford. Churches that view their relationship with their pastor as one of employer to employee have a worldly view rather than a Kingdom view. There are aspects of running a church that resemble running a small business, for sure, but it goes far beyond that!

Do we truly believe that God is actively involved in the process of calling a pastor to come and serve in a particular church or ministry? The church prays that God will provide the spiritual leadership the people of God need at this point in their life and ministry. The pastor prays that God will place him or her in a community where they can faithfully serve and love the people, helping them grow in their faith and ministry. Who but Christ, the head of the Church, knows what the congregation *really needs* in order to be challenged to grow and develop to be more like Christ and more effective in ministry? Who but Christ truly knows the community of faith among whom a pastor can not only effectively bring his or her established strengths and gifts but also be challenged by God to continue to grow and develop?

A Kingdom view of pastor to congregation is one that suggests mutual ministry. Pastor serves congregation, and congregation serves pastor, just as Jesus directed each of us to serve one another in love. In this way, we *all* continue to learn and grow in our discipleship of Jesus and to function fully as the "priesthood of *all* believers" (1 Peter 2:5-9).

Churches and pastors must remember that though they may actively seek and find God's leading and guidance in the pastoral calling process, this is only the beginning of trusting God to reveal what He intends for the pastor's role going forward. Too often, soon after the celebration of the pastoral installation, the congregation and the pastor slip into an employer/employee relationship that is dominated by performance—just as it is in the secular workplace.

In the event that performance is found to be lacking, whether it be an unexpected delivery style, choice of topics, disagreement in theology, conflict that cannot be resolved, or otherwise unacceptable behavior, the church is tempted to proceed with ending the relationship. But in the Kingdom of God, in which citizenship is initiated and sustained in God's unconditional love and grace, performance is not the primary measure of any person.

In our churches, we often look too quickly past this divine relationship, especially when it comes to the pastors and staff in our

*God uses the health of
a pastor to help the church
and the health of a church
to help the pastor.
In caring for a pastor in
the midst of brokenness,
God is caring for the church
as well. We are all part of
one body, the Body of Christ.*

churches. We trust and believe that God has initiated the relationship, but we fail to keep God in the center of that relationship going forward. We need to regularly and prayerfully ask these four important questions:

1.   God, what do you want to do in and through this unique relationship, at this particular time, with our faith community, with our wider community, and in the heart of this spiritual leader? What is our ministry to each other and with each other?

2.   God, what larger purpose, plan, and promises do you have for this pastor and our congregation as we walk together with the Holy Spirit?

3.   God, what are the steps we should take toward your purpose, plan, and promise(s) for us?

4.   God, what areas do you need to grow in our congregation and in our pastor(s) so that we can be a more effective participant in your Kingdom?

God has already promised that He can bring good things, especially growth in our trust of Him—out of our challenges. If we believe God is faithful to His Word, then we will be confident that among the many good things He will do, He will make us more like Jesus in the inevitable relationship challenges we encounter. (Romans 8:28-30) This is His primary purpose in all that He has and will do in and among us.

Our focus as the larger Body of Christ must be to live out our relationship with God and one another by both reflecting and sustaining God's unconditional love. This is our unique and life-changing witness to the world! We don't become invisible when we are experiencing conflict and brokenness. As a matter of fact, people are watching more intently during these times. They want to see how you and your community of faith handle the difficult moments.

The divine purpose for Christ's sacrificial death and resurrection from the grave was our restoration and reconciliation, bringing life through the Holy Spirit. (1 Peter 3:18) This is given to us once and for all and also as a continuing work of the Holy Spirit. Our cracks, flaws, and distortions are all kindling for the fire that God is using to remove impurities.

Have you ever had people wonder out loud why the Church does not look much different from the world? Have you ever wondered why we can't do better? Pastors have the hardest time trying to respond to that kind of question because their sole job is to help the congregation rise above and live life with an eternal perspective.

When we pray the Lord's Prayer, found in Matthew 6:9-13, we say, "your kingdom come, your will be done, on earth as it is in heaven." Is that just a pipe dream or have the followers of Christ been uniquely positioned to display His Kingdom operating on earth in our communities and churches?

And yes, this includes the pastor as well, joining in service and partnership. We have a powerful opportunity to see the Holy Spirit unleashed in our faith communities on behalf of God's Kingdom. It is the work of the Holy Spirit that will bring forth the transforming power of God's Kingdom in our churches, homes, and communities.

REFLECTIONS ON THE JOURNEY

As a way to enter into a conversation with God about restoration, take some time to give thanks and rejoice in God's character and promise, turning to Him in faith and in love. Read the verse below and develop a Prayer, Petition, and Praise based on the chapter and verse.

Romans 8:28

"And we know that for those who love God all things work together for good, for those who are called according to his purpose."

Prayer (confession and listening) _____

_____

_____

_____

Petition (our needs) _____

_____

_____

_____

Praise (bringing Him glory) _____

_____

_____

_____

CHAPTER FIVE

GOD'S RESTORATION

We do not have to look far before we see God's gracious hand of restoration. Let's set the stage of restoration from God's perspective. There is a reason that God is called the Alpha and the Omega. He has a plan from start to finish. He knows what He started, He knew what would get twisted and misunderstood, and He knows how to make it all right.

Revelation 21:5 says, "And the one who was seated on the throne said, 'Behold, I am marking all things new.' Also he said, 'write this down, for these words are trustworthy and true.'"

God has in mind a returning to the Garden of Eden, a reversal of what got broken in humanity's sin. In Revelation 5:1-4, John sees a new heaven, a new Holy City, that has been prepared. In this new city, there is a promise that tears will be wiped away and death shall be no more. There will be no more mourning, crying, or pain because the former things have passed away. That is our future hope, but it is also our present help!

God also promised that He would never leave us or forsake us. In fact, our present help is tied to Jesus' call that we see in Isaiah 61:1-7. "The Spirit of the Lord God is upon me because the Lord has anointed me to bring good news to the poor; he has sent me to bind up the brokenhearted, to proclaim liberty to the captives, and the opening of the prison to those who are bound; to proclaim the year of the Lord's favor, and the day of vengeance of our God; to comfort all who mourn; to grant to those who mourn in Zion to give them a beautiful headdress instead of ashes, the oil of gladness instead of mourning, the garment of praise instead of a faint spirit; that they may be called oaks of righteousness, the planting of the Lord, that he may be glorified. They shall build up the ancient ruins; they shall raise up the former devastations; they shall repair the ruined cities, the devastations of many generations. Strangers shall stand and tend your flocks; foreigners shall be your plowmen and vinedressers; but you shall be called the priests of the Lord; they shall speak of you as the ministers of our God; you shall eat the wealth of the nations, and in their glory, you shall boast. Instead of your shame, there shall be a double portion; instead of dishonor they shall rejoice in their lot; therefore in their land, they shall possess a double portion; they shall have everlasting joy."

Very clearly, God is in the business of restoration. I do not think there is a person reading these words who can say there isn't some part of Jesus' call directly meant for them. The ministry of Jesus is the ministry of His followers and especially His Church!

If Christ is all of this for us, then we ought to be working to play a role in the work of Christ to deliver this kind of restoration to others. I now recognize that along the way, there are things that got out of whack, truths that were turned into lies, messages that caused harm, and foundations that were not clearly set. But God in His infinite wisdom planned for the detours of His creation. In Jesus Christ, He places the power to set things right.

Ephesians 1:10 says, "And this is the plan: At the right time he will bring everything together under the authority of Christ—everything in heaven and on earth." I could not state this on the front end of my journey through brokenness because I had too many questions for God. Why am I dealing with emotions around my childhood? Why now? The short answer is this: God's timing is perfect. He moved me in a way that I would gain great freedom and become further equipped to make a difference for His Kingdom.

Have you ever had the opportunity to watch a fancy classic car driving down the street? Every time I see one, I am amazed at the cleanliness and beauty that is still on full display so many years past its prime. However, I am also aware of what it must have taken to get the car to look that way. The restorer first had to find and purchase the old car. Then he or she had to carefully inspect and make a list of the damaged and missing parts that will need to be fixed or replaced. The rebuilding tasks were sequenced, parts found and installed. It is a process that probably required months of planning and many additional months—if not years—of actual hands-on work. As any restorer knows, the work of fine tuning and polishing is never done. It's a process of love to give an old car a new life! So it is in our lives with God. Some things take time, careful planning, and polishing, but make no mistake, God is still working on you and me!

One of the most satisfying parts of God's restoration plan is His ability to turn despair into rejoicing. To stand in a place of despair, bitterness, loss, sorrow, pain, or loneliness and have a profound sense of joy completely defies common sense. It is a gift we all long for, and it only comes by way of the miraculous work done at the hand of our King.

1 Peter 5:10 seems to indicate that God chooses when to restore. It says, "And after you have suffered a little while, the God of all grace, who has called you to his eternal glory in Christ, will himself restore, confirm, strengthen, and establish you." I have become intrigued by watching how and when God chooses restoration for those who journey through some degree of brokenness and suffering. It begs the question, does God (or should God) restore one to ministry if the person's suffering comes at the hands of personal and seemingly preventable brokenness?

Before we can even consider jumping on that train, let's make sure we understand the context of this particular scripture. I understand Peter is dealing with the notion of eternity, but there is also power for us today. Being called to His eternal glory is a reminder of our identity and God's ultimate promise in us. That means we can depend on Him for *all of the above* as we go through the ups and downs of life.

In His timing, God will make us strong, firm, and established. We may feel weak now. We can sense ourselves being worn out and diminished, watching all our opportunities and prospects shrink away. But once our God calls us home, He will restore every lost thing of value, plus so much more. He will make us strong and secure for eternity. That's His promise for us. That's what's coming, and that is, I believe, available in part, on this earth to those who put their faith in Him.

Take some time to consider the following verses:

> John 21:15-17: "When they had finished breakfast, Jesus said to Simon Peter, 'Simon, son of John, do you love me more than these?' He said to him, 'Yes, Lord; you know that I love you.' He said to him, 'Feed my lambs.' He said to him a second time, 'Simon, son

of John, do you love me?' He said to him, 'Yes, Lord; you know that I love you.' He said to him, 'Tend my sheep.' He said to him the third time, 'Simon, son of John, do you love me?' Peter was grieved because he said to him the third time, 'Do you love me?' and he said to him, 'Lord, you know everything; you know that I love you.' Jesus said to him, 'Feed my sheep.'"

Most of us are well acquainted with this text. Peter denied Jesus three times, just as Jesus had predicted. Can you imagine being that person who walked with Jesus and saw the works of His hand and yet denied the very things you saw with your own eyes? Peter denied Jesus behind His back. Jesus restored Peter after asking him the most important question of all: Do you love me?

We are Peter and Peter is us. Sometimes in our actions, inner thoughts, and in the way we choose to treat others, we deny Jesus. We fail to accept and share the abundance of the truth, grace, and love that He has so freely given to us. When we fall in our sin, we deny our King. But in His faithfulness, we are brought back into the fold as our hearts sing, *I love you, Lord*. I am thankful for a Lord who never stops looking for opportunities to draw us to himself by redeeming us, restoring us, and renewing us—every day if needed!

REFLECTIONS ON THE JOURNEY

As a way to enter into a conversation with God about restoration, take some time to give thanks and rejoice in God's character and promise, turning to Him in faith and in love. Read the verse below and develop a Prayer, Petition, and Praise based on the chapter and verse.

Isaiah 40:31

"but they who wait for the Lord shall renew their strength; they shall mount up with wings like eagles; they shall run and not be weary; they shall walk and not faint."

Prayer (confession and listening) _____

_____

_____

_____

Petition (our needs) _____

_____

_____

_____

Praise (bringing Him glory) _____

_____

_____

_____

CHAPTER SIX

THE PROCESS

Moving toward any level of restoration is a journey. It is especially hard when the world is telling the church to call it quits on their guy. But I believe that sometimes, though not always, a congregation is called to be about restoration and healing instead of parting ways. This is an uncomfortable journey for both the church and the pastor. It is important to have stops along the way that mark God's goodness and faithfulness and acknowledge and celebrate the progress that's been made.

This process could be better described as spiritual healing. I am not talking about a cure. What is the difference, you ask? As a culture, we often look for and expect quick fixes. We want results at microwave speed. We want to get things working the way they should by standards and timing *we* create, not God.

Letting God take the lead to design the steps and determine the outcome will make it possible for us to find spiritual healing. We need to be willing to take a significant look at the path that brought us to the place of brokenness. Any kind of spiritual healing starts with God. When we call on His name, we can trust that He responds out of who He is as a healer—Jehovah-Rapha—which means "the Lord who heals." Jehovah-Rapha has the power to heal spiritually, physically, emotionally, and mentally.

Isn't it comforting to know that scripture speaks to *all* the ways God heals? Any lasting and true healing is initiated, sustained, and accomplished in and through the power of God and His great love. Spiritual transformation is a powerful, soul-refreshing journey!

In 2 Corinthians 2: 5-11, Paul has something to say to the church at Corinth: "Now if anyone has caused pain, he has caused it not to me, but in some measure—not to put it too severely—to all of you. For such a one, this punishment by the majority is enough, so you should rather turn to forgive and comfort him, or he may be overwhelmed by excessive sorrow. So I beg you to reaffirm your love for him. For this is why I wrote that I might test you and know whether you are obedient in everything. Anyone whom you forgive, I also forgive. Indeed, what I have forgiven, if I have forgiven anything, has been for your sake in the presence of Christ, so that we would not be outwitted by Satan; for we are not ignorant of his designs."

Can you see what the pattern of forgiveness ought to be for the church?

1. Forgive and comfort so that the offender will not be overwhelmed by sorrow.

2. Reaffirm love for the offender.

3. Be obedient in everything . . . to the way of Jesus.

As church leaders, it's important that we not give into the deceptions and devices of Satan, such as demonizing the offender, accepting division within the body, taking sides, or participating in gossip and slander. I have been around churches that far too quickly lose sight of what Paul is describing in 2 Corinthians. When things are going well, we are fooled into thinking it is because we are running excellent programming and making visitors feel welcome. That is perhaps one of our biggest mistakes. We owe God all the glory when things go well, and if we keep our eyes on Him, it will be much easier to seek His guidance when things aren't going well.

Churches should be characterized by the way they forgive and comfort *so* that the offender does not get overwhelmed and recoil from God, the ultimate healer and restorer. And that leads us to discuss the problem. Churches move toward forgiveness but do not take it the entire way. Because in the midst of forgiving, and even comforting, there are larger conversations about demonizing, gossiping, and taking sides. Make no mistake here. This can lead the congregation into corporate sin. When churches say with their actions that they love the offender as long as they leave town, they are missing the opportunity to display God's redeeming love. Dear pastors and church leaders, it's time to take a good look at what it really means to forgive, comfort, and reaffirm. As much as humanly possible, we must strip away our feelings and selfish thoughts. I am not suggesting we become robots, but I am simply holding out the call for us to look to Jesus and obediently strive for how He wants us to proceed.

Churches, please remember that Satan is on the prowl and wants to find a way to devour us, both individually and corporately. If we are not careful to consider that Satan is in our midst, we could be misguided by the enemy and miss out on what God has been saving for us.

When things are going well, we are fooled into thinking it is because we are running excellent programming and making visitors feel welcome. That is perhaps one of our biggest mistakes. We owe God all the glory when things go well, and if we keep our eyes on Him, it will be much easier to seek His guidance when things aren't going well.

Does this all sound great, especially since you aren't being tested with any brokenness or disagreements at the moment in your congregation? If so, then you are in the perfect spot to be creating a process by which you will deal with brokenness or disagreements, not *if*, but *when* they come. In general, churches seem ignorant to the fact that pastors carry into any job a certain amount of baggage. And the vast majority have not thought through how they will care for their pastors should an issue arise, small or big.

A church should start by establishing support for their pastor from the outset, as they serve the whole person, including spiritual, mental, emotional, social, and physical health. Most churches leave it up to the pastor to find the care and support he/she needs outside of the congregation and on their own time. It's a common mindset that many well-meaning elder boards have never considered or questioned.

It's time we flip the script.

As we seek to help our pastor, our church may have to face some of our own uncomfortable truths, unresolved conflicts, and brokenness within the congregation that need to be repented of, forgiven, reconciled, and healed. As a church, we have a vertical connection with Jesus Christ, which gives us a call to be healing communities. Because of our connection to Christ, we work by the grace of God to live out Isaiah 61:1: "He has sent me to bind up the brokenhearted. The spirit of the Lord is on me because he has anointed me to preach good news to the poor." This also includes how we care for pastors. It is not a church and a pastor, but rather the pastor is *part of* the church.

It is part of our human nature to be drawn to community. In so doing, we can find our tribe where we feel like we belong and can offer that sense of belonging to others as well. When we are not part of a healthy community who affirms truth in us, we can count on the fact there will be unhealthy distortions.

Margaret Josephson Rinck's 1992 article called "Becoming a Healing Community" was reprinted as a *Christianity Today* Classic in August 2000. In the article, Rinck reported that her church's Teleios Ministry helps believers feel better equipped to offer help to the hurting through empathetic listening skills, combined with biblical teaching on relationships. She writes, "To help people recover from sin and failure's wounds, we need to create a community where it is acceptable to be broken, have problems, admit failure, and where help is expressed in concrete, practical ways. Where each day any one can seek out wholeness, significance, and happiness which cannot be met outside of being a part of a strong faith community. In my very biased opinion, this includes the pastor. After all, pastors are only human." [5]

Although it is not the one and only process, I want to offer it simply and humbly by way of my own experience and observations. What is most important is that a process is put in place so *any* person in the church community experiencing brokenness will have members of their church ready and willing to step into it and walk beside them.

You may not know yet what role you will play in this process, but if you prepare with a posture toward the journey by giving yourself fully over to God, you will be ready to accept help or stand alongside someone else who needs help.

Take some time to consider Proverbs 3:5-8: "Trust in the Lord with all your heart, and do not lean on your own understanding. In all your ways acknowledge him, and he will make straight your paths. Be not wise in your own eyes; fear the Lord and turn away from evil. It will be healing to your flesh and refreshment to your bones."

Wherever there is a place of brokenness, you will also find that there is a level of giving in to your own understanding. I know this was true for me. Romans 12:2 says, "Do not be conformed to this

In general, churches seem ignorant to the fact that pastors carry into any job a certain amount of baggage. And the vast majority have not thought through how they will care for their pastors should an issue arise, small or big.

world, but be transformed by the renewal of your mind, that by testing you may discern what is the will of God, what is good and acceptable and perfect." We tend to not give enough attention to the first part of the text. It is clear that we are to be transformed *by the renewing of our minds.*

Note the first seven words of the verse: "Do not be conformed to this world." Conforming to this world includes thinking as the world thinks rather than staying grounded in what God says. We all fall prey to thinking about ourselves according to how the world says we should be valued. We listen to what others have to say about who we are and how we ought to act. This is wrong thinking but so easy to do! Personal transformation is found in who God says we are. In Christ, we have great value.

Take my dyslexia for example. I have, for the most part, adjusted to it, but that doesn't mean I'm glad I have it. Every time I sit down to read a book or write a sermon, I am painfully reminded of my disability. The world, not God, says good preachers read a book a week. Here is the reality for me. I can't read a book a week, but that doesn't mean I can't read books more slowly or listen to them on audio. The world wants me to feel badly about this, but when God called me to be a pastor, He didn't put such demands on me. He wanted to use my life experiences to touch the lives of others. God called me with my dyslexia—possibly *because* of my dyslexia.

I had been fighting a battle against the world's standards my whole life. What I have learned and want so desperately to explain to other people is that we were never meant to fight that battle. God has a vision for how he will use each one of us, and that vision includes all of our strengths and weaknesses. The very thing that I saw as broken, the thing that eventually led me to use the words of others in my sermons, was the thing that God wanted to use to demonstrate His power, grace, and mercy to me and to others.

Though we don't necessarily have control over our limitations, disabilities, or life circumstances, God has a plan for how to use all of it to reach and encourage others for His glory. I do not know if I would have ever understood this without being open to restoration and healing. I entered a process that included surrendering all that I understand about myself, including my dyslexia, and fully expecting that the Holy Spirit is at work, helping me to see myself as my Father sees me.

Here is a list of important elements for the process your church or ministry will create. If your church is in a healthy stage, then now is the perfect time to talk and think about this! Take the time to meet together, pray, talk, agree, and write down specific guidelines and boundaries by which you will operate should you have a situation of brokenness on your pastoral staff or in your lay leadership. Remember, for now, it isn't about the people in current leadership, it's about how your church body or ministry wants to seek restoration, aid the personal healing process for individuals, and show the grace and love of Jesus Christ. For the church or non-profit ministry that wants to do a better job of coming alongside brokenness in their faith community, in particular their leaders, I hope this is a helpful starting place.

1. **Humility**—There needs to be a heart of humility on all sides. Some leaders are naturally humble, some have to work at it more. Regardless, if it is a character quality that is valued, modeled, and expected, it will be present in your leadership.

2. **Belonging**—The pastor must be seen as part of the faith community of believers. Humility plays a huge role in the sense of a belonging a pastor feels. If the pastor is approachable and humble, the congregation will feel a greater connection to him or her during tough times.

3. **Resistance**—A church should resist moving on from a pastor too quickly. Planning to have steady leadership in times of crisis goes a long way toward being able to achieve this when things get complicated.

4. **Pursuit of God**—Everyone should be pursuing their walk with God. This is central to the health of every church. All your efforts in encouraging meaningful Bible studies, worship, and prayer will help keep you centered in times of crisis.

5. **Care Teams**—The best teams have members from both inside and outside of the church. Establishing one now during a healthy time in your church is important. Anywhere from five to ten people with at least a couple from outside the church is a good goal. Meet twice a year to stay connected and review your process should a situation arise.

6. **Make Room**—A time apart may be needed for the necessary healing work. Consider the pros

and cons of this strategy and how God might
be glorified through making room for a pause.
Define in a broader sense what a pause might
look like versus an immediate resignation or
firing. It will help you make a better choice when
you are faced with that difficult decision.

A process is only as good as the commitment to it. It should be
clearly understood that any process will take time and be a step of
faith. God will provide the time and space to facilitate healing wherever hearts are open to the process. It will require faith because the
ultimate outcome cannot be known at the onset. With that said, I
think it is okay and important to put some semi-flexible parameters
on the duration of the process. If you earnestly lean into the God of
hope and healing, He will bring about a divine outcome in the lives
of those who are on the journey. When we bow our human spirit to
be in the posture of, "Here I am, Lord," we receive peace, love, and
acceptance for *all* of who we are right now and who we are becoming
in Christ our Lord.

REFLECTIONS ON THE JOURNEY

As a way to enter into a conversation with God about restoration, take some time to give thanks and rejoice in God's character and promise, turning to Him in faith and in love. Read the verse below and develop a Prayer, Petition, and Praise based on the chapter and verse.

Proverbs 3:5-8

"Trust in the Lord with all your heart, and do not lean on your own understanding. In all your ways acknowledge him, and he will make straight your paths. Be not wise in your own eyes; fear the Lord, and turn away from evil. It will be healing to your flesh and refreshment to your bones."

Prayer (confession and listening) _____

_____

_____

_____

Petition (our needs) _____

_____

_____

_____

Praise (bringing Him glory) _____

_____

_____

_____

CHAPTER SEVEN

HUMILITY

When you consider creating a process that can lead to restoration (for both pastor and congregation), the best starting place is a mindset that is humble and teachable. That's why I made it #1 on my list of what a good process will contain. You might think I am talking to pastors, but make no mistake, humility is an important standard for the entire church. *All* involved in the process need to be humble and teachable before God and show His grace to one another.

But how can you tell if someone is humble or not? True humility is not absent of confidence, but rather, the confidence is securely rooted in our true identity in Christ. True humility is a work of the Holy Spirit! "Humility is the key to progress. If we are of this same humble mindset, forsaking our reputation and honor to be obedient to God's Word and will, we will be able to make unbelievable progress in our Christian lives!" said Nellie Owens in her article called "4 Things Everyone Should Know About Humility," posted on www.activechristianity.org.[6]

When an issue or an area of brokenness has come to light, humility must be evident in order to move forward in the process of healing and restoration. It is a frame of mind that should be a part of our daily walk, not added in as needed.

On www.unlockingthebible.org, Colton Tatham says that humbleness is about submission, mourning, repentance, and prayer.[7] I can personally share that each of these four characteristics of humbleness became real and evident in my life during the time I came face-to-face with my brokenness. They did not come all at once, and they weren't all four out on public display, but they were each felt very deeply.

These four characteristics of humbleness can be found in James 4:6-10, which says, "God opposes the proud but gives grace to the humble. Submit yourselves therefore to God. Resist the devil, and he will flee from you. Draw near to God, and he will draw near to you. Humble yourselves before the Lord, and he will exalt you."

No matter how great the process, it will not be able to run its course and do its work if a person isn't willing to say, "There is something in me that needs correcting." This leads us to the next, most important step: being teachable.

We can only begin to become aware of our blind spots if we are willing to allow someone to point them out. Once a blind spot is pointed out, we need a Spirit-filled person to be our journey companion—teaching and coaching us to deal with the areas of brokenness through the transforming power of the Holy Spirit and Jesus, the *healer* of brokenness.

No matter the issue, it is rarely just about the one area the spotlight was placed on. It is about the areas of brokenness that led up to the moment of exposure as well. I had a great prayer counselor during this time in my life. One of the things he taught me that will forever stay active in my life is that there is a progression that leads up to the moment of revelation of brokenness.

In my journey toward healing, I discovered that there were some areas in my life experiences that needed just as much work, if not more, than my present area of brokenness. Some areas totally surprised me, while others I was already aware of at some level. I was amazed by how much my past had a hold on me. With a spirit of humility, I began to work on releasing the power of its grip.

I say this as a person who has lived with 2 Corinthians 3:17 as both my life and mission verse: "Now the Lord is the Spirit, and where the Spirit of the Lord is, there is freedom." I have lived my life and pastored out of this verse. Through my prayer counselor, I discovered that the freedom of 2 Corinthians 3:17 had not reached some areas in my life experience that needed saving, healing, freedom.

I could not have learned or processed any of this without God using someone to mentor me through it. Once a person has submitted, mourned, repented, and prayed, it's helpful to have someone remind you that God has promised the old things are gone and the new has come! God be praised for faithfully healing the humble heart.

Rick Warren says in his book, *The Purpose Driven Life*, "True humility is not thinking less of yourself; it is thinking of yourself less."[8] Humility requires a certain amount of introspection, self-control, and self-esteem. These *all* come from God! They are received in daily abiding in Him. Our growth comes from trusting in the truth of what God says about us, being constantly thankful to Him for our true identity and staying ever aware of His complete care and protection of our hearts. Understanding who we are from God's perspective *frees* us to turn our primary focus on Him and all those we are called to be in relationship with through His love.

God's got us completely covered!

It will be a lifelong endeavor of growth for pastors hoping to shepherd people well. Leading a faith community is incredibly hard. Your self-awareness and trustworthiness are often tested as you work to be the leader God called you to be.

Here are three ways to grow humility within yourself.

1. **Accept your humanness.**

   This may well be one of the hardest to attempt. We want to be perceived as having it all together. Many expect us to have it all together. But the reality is that we are human; we are all flawed. That is our starting place, not perfection. It comes down to our willingness to let people see our imperfections.

2. **Compassion for ourselves.**

   We can be hard on ourselves. We can see the flaws we have and at the same time not give ourselves grace. Give yourself permission to be okay with failing on that project; know that you are not the only person falling short or the only one who doesn't have it all together. Find ways to be encouraged.

3. **Gratitude, gratitude, gratitude.**

   Well-known pastor and author, James MacDonald, said, "Gratitude is the attitude that sets the altitude for living."[9] Give yourself the time to be grateful for what you have, the gifts that have been given to you, and the people who love you, encourage you, and challenge you to step into the freedom that God has given through Christ Jesus.

Why is gratitude so central to the process? Because when we are thanking God and rejoicing in God, we can't help but get our focus off ourselves and turn it (repent) fully in God's direction. In the midst of this, God ministers, encourages, heals, inspires, empowers, and humbles us in the most life-giving, *uplifting* way!

We don't need a rah-rah pep talk, we need to declare God's truth about ourselves, daily. Say this out loud with me:

> *I am beloved. I am a new creation in Christ. God says I am worthy, and He knows me better than anyone, including myself! He delights in me. His joy is over me, and what I am learning and becoming is my strength.*

And as we declare this, God will confirm in our heart and establish the reality in our lives by empowering us to think and act according to His truth.

Take some time to consider 2 Chronicles 7:14: "If my people who are called by my name humble themselves and pray and seek my face and turn from their wicked ways, then I will hear from heaven and will forgive their sin and heal their land."

You can't own your stuff without being humble. Taking responsibility for what we need to own is one of the most important steps in our healing journey. When we humble ourselves, God begins to heal the brokenness found in the landscape of our lives.

In this text, God tells us He is waiting on us to get a grip on where we are in the situation of our brokenness. I do not want to understate God's desire to bring healing. In the book of Genesis, Adam is told to stay away from the fruit, yet he eats it anyway. Soon after, Adam is hiding from God. Walking through the garden, God calls out to Adam with a question, "Where are you, Adam?"

Think about it. Did God pose the question because He really did not know where Adam was? I think not! God knew exactly where Adam was. God wanted Adam to admit why he was hiding, naked, and ashamed. Adam owned up to what he had done to a certain extent. He honestly admitted that he hid when he heard God approaching. Yet he did not own the actual sin itself which was disobeying God by eating the fruit. He blamed Eve for that! Adam rationalized his choice to sin by focusing on his circumstances instead of the actual sin itself. Adam did not own his part.

There will always be circumstances that go along with feelings of being ashamed, embarrassed, lost, out of control, or just plain guilty. Trust me, I know from my own journey. But take heart, we have a God who stands ready to hear our cry, grant us forgiveness, and deliver healing as we seek after Him. How amazing is that? As we go through life, and especially as we help others through the process of healing and restoration, we need to continually remind ourselves of this incredible gift.

When I was in the darkest moments at the start of my healing journey, I needed to rediscover the Heavenly Father in the garden. Not only was He waiting for me, but He was also drawing himself to me. He knew what I had done. I was ashamed, yet I desired to be near Him. God is also there in the garden, ready to embrace and help us. Once we humble ourselves before God, it is only a matter of time before healing will begin. Do not lose this point. Allow the full weight of its power to rest on you. Our God is in the business of delivering on His promises, and He wants to bring healing in the areas of our brokenness.

We may do the very thing He told us not to do. We may be like Paul, wondering why we do the things we don't want to do and don't do the things we want to do. No matter what the case may be, there are no surprises that catch God sleeping on the job. His response remains the same: "Come to me, all you who are weary and burdened, and I will give you rest" (Matthew 11:28). In our weakest moments, God remains strong and steadfast in His commitment and love toward us. "But God shows his love for us in that while we were still sinners, Christ died for us" (Romans 5:8). Often, we have to go through the fire in life in order to see or be reminded that we are in the arms of a loving God.

REFLECTIONS ON THE JOURNEY

As a way to enter into a conversation with God about restoration, take some time to give thanks and rejoice in God's character and promise, turning to Him in faith and in love. Read the verse below and develop a Prayer, Petition, and Praise based on the chapter and verse.

2 Chronicles 7:14

"If my people who are called by my name humble themselves, and pray and seek my face and turn from their wicked ways, then I will hear from heaven and will forgive their sin and heal their land."

Prayer (confession and listening) _____

_____

_____

_____

Petition (our needs) _____

_____

_____

_____

Praise (bringing Him glory) _____

_____

_____

_____

CHAPTER EIGHT

KINGDOM CARE TEAMS

We do not have to read the Bible for long before discovering that Scripture has lots to add to a discussion relating to caring for one another. 1 Peter 1:22-23 calls on us to come around someone with care: "Having purified your souls by your obedience to the truth for sincere brotherly love, love one another earnestly from a pure heart, since you have been born again, not of perishable seed but of imperishable, through the living and abiding word of God."

Once we have been touched by the transforming truth of our living God, we are called to respond in ways that are different from how the world would respond. Too often, Christians don't follow God's call to be different, and that is why the world is left wondering what we're all about.

In Ephesians 4:32, we find words that are simply too hard to look away from: "Be kind to one another, tenderhearted, forgiving one another, as God in Christ forgave you." Let's make sure we set the record straight. We all are a mess to some degree. Your mess is no greater than my mess. It all smells the same and is seen in the same way by our Lord. Jesus died and wiped the record clean, for you and for me. In the Bible verse above, God encourages us to approach one another, no matter the size or kind of mess it may be. We are to do so tenderheartedly and forgive as God has done for each of us.

And did you notice it says, "Christ forgave you?" That's past tense. Yes, that means that when He forgives, the forgiveness is done. It's in the past! Likewise, although much harder for us at times, we are called to forgive others in the same way God forgives us. . .by leaving it in the past.

The Bible tells us that God extended His love, care, and forgiveness, while we were yet sinners. That means we need a Kingdom Care Team, or we need to serve on one so we stand ready and able to remind each other of God's radical, crazy, transforming love.

Everyone needs people who will surround them with care, support, and encouragement. This took shape for me in two forms. I was blessed to have a group of pastors committed to meeting together for three years. We met regularly to pray, study, retreat, and we even traveled to Israel. These were men I did not know well before we began. Each was from a different faith perspective, and yet we had the strong, common bond of being sold out for the transforming power of Jesus Christ.

During the time that my brokenness came to light, one of the most difficult things I had to do was retell the story of what I had done to this group of pastor friends. These were relatively new relationships, and I had no idea what to expect. How would they receive the news? What would they think of me? Would I ever stand in their midst as a fellow pastor again? There were all kinds of questions running laps in my mind. I did not even know if I could get the words to roll off my tongue, but I knew I had to look them in the eye and fully own what I had done. Moments like these are where the rubber meets the road in our faith journey. As a follower of Christ, I had to confess my actions before this group of brothers I had committed to journeying with through ministry and life. As followers of Christ, they had to decide how they would not only receive my news, but also how they would treat me as a colleague and friend.

The group took my news with caring hearts and received me with love. We had conversations about my brokenness and found a common ground of understanding. Most importantly, we set Christ as the foundation of our conversation.

We can all have different reactions to any news, based on our own life experiences and perspective, but we all need to strive for the perspective of who we are in Christ, who the other person is in Christ, and what Christ might be calling each of us to do at that moment. This is not always easy to do because after all, there are just certain situations where we deserve, or think we deserve, to be angry or judgmental. But when we work to see things through God's eyes, we see that our righteousness might not be so righteous. I dare say that when we apply a Christ-like perspective to any circumstance, we will be challenged to a new way of thinking and/or experiencing the circumstance. I am thankful that this pastoral group was a safe place for me.

The second care group that helped me through my healing journey came out of my denomination. Three pastors were invited to form a care team after I stepped down from the church. I was under the care of our denomination's ordination governing body. These were people I had previously met and were part of the same denominational conference.

Once again, I found myself in that place of needing to retell the story of what had occurred. There is something that takes place when you retell your story of brokenness. Each time, I found that the weight

We can all have different reactions to any news, based on our own life experiences and perspective, but we all need to strive for the perspective of who we are in Christ, who the other person is in Christ, and what Christ might be calling each of us to do at that moment.

of the burden of brokenness became just a bit lighter. Undeniably, at the moment, you prepare to tell the story to a new group of people, you find yourself needing to deal with some of the same emotions of self-doubt, fear of judgment and rejection, and notions of being in a prison of your own design.

As I shared what I had done with this care group, these brothers offered understanding and reminders of how important I am to God. They became my accountability partners for staying on track with my self-care plan. As we met each month, I shared a bit about where my emotions had been, what I was working on, and what I still needed to do. I am thankful for a denomination that cared enough about me to suggest that a group like this be formed. God used them to help me stay grounded in my faith and believe in myself during a hard time.

There are five important reasons for having a Kingdom Care Team to care for you on your journey:

1. **You are not alone.**
   When you are trying to confront something or bring about real change in your life, it can be a lonely experience. It's easy to feel as if you are the only person dealing with it. The truth is that you are not alone. Your situation is not singular, and you are not the only person dealing with some level of brokenness.

2. **It is important to express your feelings.**
   This was and still is a difficult one for me. I would bet that many of you feel the same way. As an African American, I was taught that you "don't put your business in the streets." But I do know it is important to share your feelings with people you trust. It is

important so that you can be freed from the captivity of what can feel like death on the inside. In expressing your feelings, they become a little more real, defined, and understood, which allows you to form a game plan to deal with those deeply held emotions.

3. **Kingdom Care Teams will lend helpful information.**

I cannot even begin to tell you how much information I have gained from my care groups. I have had books placed before me that I would never have come across on my own. They helped me think about the situation differently and provided words of encouragement that cut right through the scar tissue on my heart.

4. **Others play a key role in a renewed self-understanding.**

We can be our own biggest critics. There is so much truth in this for me. No one has to beat me down, because I do a good job of that myself! Having people around you, along with the truth of God's Word, helps to get your thinking back into a proper perspective.

5. **It's essential to reduce your level of distress.**

As I worked through issues and concerns in my care groups, I began to notice a great reduction of overall distress and discomfort. This was a positive outcome. Progress was being made, hope had set in, and stress was settling into a healthier range.

The last part of my valuable, collective care team was my dear friend, Ted, whom I met several years ago while co-pastoring a church. He is a mighty man of God. Ted and his wife were part of a small group my wife and I hosted in our home. He was one of the first people I called to share the news of the upheaval in my life. After talking things over with me and encouraging me, Ted asked just one important question: "What can I do to help?"

Help from our friend, Ted, came in two forms. He drove from Tennessee to Illinois to be with me for an afternoon and to sit with me as I took part in a meeting with my denomination's Board of Ordination. This was one of the most stressful moments in my life. A decision from this board would determine my future as a pastor. Ted also called me every week after that meeting not only to check in on me, but also to talk through the Word of God with me. He reminded me that I was able to hear God speaking through His Word to me. I am thankful for God's provision for me at a time when I needed it most.

Every part of my broader care team was an important factor to my healing process. I whole heartedly suggest to pastors and church leaders that this is an area that should not be skipped over. In addition to forming a Kingdom Care Team to come alongside a pastor or staff person, I suggest churches go the extra step of putting together a care team for the church as a whole too. Churches, just like individuals, should not do ministry in isolation but rather in partnership. Forming these life-giving partnerships in times of health and stability can enable a church to receive care from another church in times of great turmoil and uncertainty. That's why I call this Kingdom Care. It is about building and supporting the Body of Christ. The days of isolation—for pastor and church alike—have to come to an end. Isolation weakens and tears down the Kingdom that we have worked to strengthen. When we stand together, the pathway to healing runs through our willingness to let people share in our pain.

For those who may have had a similar upbringing to me, while independence is not a bad quality, we have to be willing to be vulnerable and seek care when we need it. We are not alone on an island, nor do we have to man/woman up and deal with it on our own. The Kingdom of God is designed to live and grow in a community. Dare I say that if we are not opening ourselves to a faith community, we are being disobedient.

Take some time to consider the following verses in Galatians 6:1-5: "Brothers, if anyone is caught in any transgression, you who are spiritual should restore him in a spirit of gentleness. Keep watch on yourself, lest you to be tempted. Bear one another's burdens, and so fulfill the law of Christ. For if anyone thinks he is something, when he is nothing, he deceives himself. But let each one test his own work, and then his reason to boast will be in himself alone and not in his neighbor. For each will have to bear his own load."

The truth of these verses played out for me many times as I sought healing. I sometimes think that as Christ-followers, we have forgotten or lost who we are called to be within the larger Body of Christ. Or can it be that as a follower of Christ, we do not trust that the Body of Christ can fulfill its intended function? There is a sacred space that resides in the community of believers. It is a space where restoration can be found. It starts with extending a hand when a brother or sister is in need.

When I was in college, I went swimming with some friends at a nearby lake. We decided to swim out to a floating dock. I jumped in the water with everyone else and began swimming toward the dock. I wasn't too far from the floating dock when every muscle in my body shouted in unison, "Shutting down will commence in 3, 2, 1."

I started to go down.

Had it not been for my friend who noticed I was in trouble and gave me her hand, my life would have been lost that day.

The Body of Christ is meant to be that hand for one another. Galatians 6:2 tells us that we are to bear one another's burdens. When we do, we are fulfilling what Christ calls us to do. We are more like Christ in the moments where we are a community for one another.

Let us not forget that one day we may find ourselves in a moment of brokenness and in need of people to help bear our heavy load. Likewise, we may find ourselves needing to serve on someone's care team, coming alongside them in their journey from brokenness to restoration. It is a trick of the evil one to try and convince us that we are alone and should live on the outside of the community where we once belonged. Churches should beware of the pervasive, mainstream mindset that a pastor experiencing brokenness should be able to manage without much outside help. Let us connect to people in a way where we help others cast their burdens on the Lord (Psalm 55:22) with the understanding that He will sustain us. God is our refuge.

REFLECTIONS ON THE JOURNEY

As a way to enter into a conversation with God about restoration, take some time to give thanks and rejoice in God's character and promise, turning to Him in faith and in love. Read the verse below and develop a Prayer, Petition, and Praise based on the chapter and verse.

John 13:34-35

"A new commandment I give to you, that you love one another: just as I have loved you, you also are to love one another. By this all people will know that you are my disciples, if you have love for one another."

Prayer (confession and listening) _____

_____

_____

_____

Petition (our needs) _____

_____

_____

_____

Praise (bringing Him glory) _____

_____

_____

_____

CHAPTER NINE

GROWTH

There are times when we all need help personally or professionally. The first time I recognized that I needed help was during my church planting years. In the midst of trying to lead a church plant, it became clear that I had too much on my plate. I was trying to grow from scratch a multi-ethnic church focused on a low-income population. Any church planting is especially challenging, but I probably took on more challenges than most. I was determined for good reason; God had called me to do this great work for His Kingdom!

A couple of years into the church plant, I felt that I needed some extra help. That's when I met a man named Tim Roehl. I heard him speak and was able to connect with him over the course of several months. He walked me through his G.R.O.W. process which is explained in his book that he co-authored with Steve Ogne, *TransforMissional Coaching*.[10] Through our conversations, Tim coached me in leading my baby church plant. Every time we met, he would ask four simple questions. I share them here with permission:

1. What is the **G**oal for our time together?

2. What is the **R**eality of what is happening?

3. What are the **O**ptions I have?

4. What **W**ill I need to get done?

Each of these questions, and others, would help me dig a little deeper. He would never give me the answer, but he would guide me along a path where I would identify my response. I am so thankful for the time that I had with Tim. It was an extremely powerful and productive time in my life.

In every setting of pastoring since this time, I have used Roehl's G.R.O.W. process to help get unstuck. The process has had such an impact on me that I have even adopted it into my pastoral counseling. I can't even begin to tell you how many times I've been blessed to see growth where people have been stuck for years. I've witnessed growth in people's jobs and careers, growth in marriages on the brink of divorce, growth in students, and even growth in churches that seemed too unhealthy to change.

During the aftermath of my brokenness, I asked myself the question, "What is the Goal?" I had to better understand what led me to this moment. "What is the Reality?" I had to step in and own my brokenness. "What are my Options?" This created a big lightbulb moment for me. I needed to find a way to move the story, the experience of all that had occurred, from the inside to the outside. This book is partly an act of obedience in doing just that. For the last question, "What will I need to get done?" I did not know what the answer would be until I put it down on paper. I just felt that there was an opportunity, not only to share my journey, but also to speak to the larger Body of Christ with the heart of a pastor who sees a vision for how we can do better.

The message is fairly simple. There is room enough within God's churches that a wounded or broken pastor should—whenever possible—be offered an opportunity and the necessary support to participate in biblical healing and restoration. This is central to the purpose of the Body of Christ.

I do not know if I would have come to a place of seeing this opportunity to find personal healing and a new freedom to love and accept myself as God does had I not entered into a full and rigorous process of self-reflection. Recognizing the brokenness, thanking God for it, seeing God's truth of who I am, and understanding how He has uniquely gifted me, has set me free to be an instrument for the continued building of His Kingdom.

While we are on this somewhat unpredictable journey, we seek to listen for the place(s) that God is speaking. It is usually more than we would have guessed, simply because we are not in the habit of listening to his voice. At one point, I realized that I had slowly lost my belief that God had anointed me. I felt broken, imperfect, and lost. During the healing process I went through, God spoke and affirmed that He is still using me for His Kingdom work. God has given me a special conviction to speak out.

The promise that I must hold tightly to is Luke 12:12 where it says, "for the Holy Spirit will teach you in that very hour what you ought to say." God is with me, and God is with you. I am actively shedding the feelings and thought patterns that have kept me from stepping into my full calling.

If anyone is going to work their way through a restorative process, it has to include some important ingredients. I learned from Tim Roehl that when I am coaching or counseling someone, I have to listen, care, and celebrate people and their ministry while being attentive to where God is working.

If you were to ask most therapists or counselors, they would tell you that the learning and healing that occurs during their sessions happens in large part because of the effort of the person being counseled. Walking through this process helped me develop much better self-awareness. I did this while, at the same time, seeing a therapist who helped me identify skills I possessed that I could use to help myself going forward. Introspection, effort, and expert help all proved to be of great help to me.

Some of you may be saying to yourself that there is no way you would ever see a therapist. I get that. After all, who wants to go and put your business in front of someone? I grew up with this frowned upon as well. Let me offer you something to consider, though. As I looked into seeing a therapist, I needed to know how the therapist moved people toward healing and if they lived their personal and professional life with a genuine Christian mindset. In going through recovery, I came across an article by Victoria Maxwell entitled, "The 6 Steps of Healing You Need to Know."[11] Although described as a sequential process, I think it's more accurately pictured or understood as a woven tapestry. When one part of the tapestry is restored, all aspects of the piece shift and improve.

Here are the six steps as named by Victoria Maxwell:

1. **Acceptance**—If we are unable to grow in knowledge and acceptance of where we are amid the circumstance, our freedom will remain far off. Denial of the brokenness is the greatest barrier, and acceptance is the liberator that awaits us.

2. **Insight**—Being open to the fact that there may be something out of balance allows healing to begin. Even the smallest degree of admission allows insight to begin.

3. **Action**— Planning each step of the healing journey will bring additional support. At each stage of insight, there can be a plan of action to move toward recovery or to find the steps needed to enlist additional support.

4. **Self-Esteem**—As positive movement is made, self-awareness will increase. Choices are made, and those decisions and actions will impact overall health and our sense of personal competency, effectiveness, and self-esteem.

5. **Healing**—Healing is about bringing what has been living in the dark into the light so that positive action steps can be taken. It is a natural byproduct of facing, rather than hiding, brokenness and taking concrete actions to address it.

6 **Meaning**—As healing occurs, a new experience with God will emerge, giving way to new insight, new vision for self, and new opportunities for God's glory to be seen working in and through us. This allows us to return to a new wholeness, complete with new experiences and new choices.

God is delighted in our efforts and desperately wants to be in the midst of the process. He alone brings lasting, eternal healing and supernatural insight and understanding. During my healing process, I had many familiar verses come alive with new meaning. I had heard countless times, and even taught on them, but this time, it was different. I heard God speaking as he uncovered truths that spoke to thoughts and feelings I thought I could hide from God.

Pastors, if you find yourself in a moment of brokenness, and if your leadership team or church is willing to walk through it with you, I want to encourage you to consider making a plan for your healing process. Always include people who you know will speak into your life. Churches, when brokenness comes to light in the life of one of your pastors, I want to encourage you to rest on your commitment to your pastor. Work on establishing an initial care team before you do anything else. This will go a long way toward helping your pastor find restorative healing, whether they stay for the long term or leave.

Take some time to consider the following verses. Psalm 92:12-14: "The righteous flourish like the palm tree and grow like a cedar in Lebanon. They are planted in the house of the LORD; they flourish in the courts of our God. They still bear fruit in old age; they are ever full of sap and green."

Our walk—our journey—with Christ should be filled with areas of continual growth. There is no time or situation in our lives that does not bring with it the potential to grow and mature in our relationship with God and in our ability to effectively contribute to the building of His Kingdom. Going through a time of healing is certainly one of those opportunities.

I have found that the *reason* I didn't initially embrace the need for healing was because I was ashamed and fearful. I kept trying in my own power to bring my own healing, but it was superficial at best.

God is truly overjoyed to step in and take charge of the necessary learning and relearning in order to bring lasting change.

My experience changed my feelings about facing brokenness, and I now view it in a radically different way. A major component of my healing has been the full acceptance of my dyslexia. It is the very thing God used to reveal that my effectiveness as a pastor is not rooted in my performance, but rather in the truth of God's love. In that context, dyslexia is a gift!

By God's beautiful grace, my faith has grown by leaps and bounds. Our low times are low. Sadly, they can be very low. I felt kicked in the gut, knocked upside the head, and my heart ripped out all at the same time. I felt low, lost, ashamed, and yes, alone. No matter the brokenness or sin, so long as the person has a degree of humility, these feelings will be pretty universal. Take heart, my fellow believers. When God is on the throne, He picks up His children and turns our focus to the person God sees. This is what "lifted up as a child of His glory" means to me now. Transgressions have been removed, and God's promise that He will never forsake us remains true and steady. He does not waste a moment of our experiences. Aren't we so grateful for this? By the power of the Holy Spirit, He gets us going straight again.

I like to say we have a "U-turn God." When we are faithful to trust in His care, even when we mess up, He facilitates healing and works it out for His glory. I am determined to flourish like a cedar in Lebanon! My journey has given me a better glimpse of all that God means to me as I seek His plans for my life.

We cannot grow if we do not set a goal, be clear on our reality, seek after the best options for help, and chart our way on what we will do next. I did not know if I could make it back from my feelings of despair. Some days, all I could do is take one step. After I took a

Take heart, my fellow believers.
When God is on the throne,
He picks up His children and turns
our focus to the person God sees.
This is what "lifted up as a child
of His glory" means to me now.
Transgressions have been removed,
and God's promise that
He will never forsake us remains
true and steady. He does not waste
a moment of our experiences.
Aren't we so grateful for this?
By the power of the Holy Spirit,
He gets us going straight again.

baby step, I found that God was already there, lovingly waiting for me. God is so faithful!

How about you? Are you willing to take a step of faith? Are you in a position to encourage someone who is hurting, ashamed, embarrassed, or upset to take just one step in the right direction? If they take the step, God will be there.

REFLECTIONS ON THE JOURNEY

As a way to enter into a conversation with God about restoration, take some time to give thanks and rejoice in God's character and promise, turning to Him in faith and in love. Read the verse below and develop a Prayer, Petition, and Praise based on the chapter and verse.

Colossians 1:9-10

"And so, from the day we heard, we have not ceased to pray for you, asking that you may be filled with the knowledge of his will in all spiritual wisdom and understanding, so as to walk in a manner worthy of the Lord, fully pleasing to him: bearing fruit in every good work and increasing in the knowledge of God."

Prayer (confession and listening) _____

_____

_____

_____

Petition (our needs) _____

_____

_____

_____

Praise (bringing Him glory) _____

_____

_____

_____

CHAPTER TEN

HEALING SABBATH

Some years back, when I was in seminary, I had the opportunity to spend some time in Zimbabwe, Africa. Victoria Falls, on the border of Zimbabwe and Zambia, is one of the most beautiful places on earth. Feeling the spray of the waterfall on my face and arms before I reached the full view, I had a profound and unforgettable moment. The locals call the spray from the waterfall, "smoke that thunders."

It was a moment that I felt the presence of God. The mist was thick and falling on my face. I began to dance and jump around—not something I would ordinarily do! My travel companions thought I had lost my mind. When asked what I was doing, I replied, "I'm dancing for my Jesus!"

In that moment, I felt at peace and at rest with everything. I felt like I fully understood God's call for us to rest, and to find Him in restful moments. Stopping in that moment and sensing the presence of God was nothing like I had felt before. It was a "Sabbath moment."

Now, we know that Sabbath means to rest or to cease and that God calls us to it. Exodus 20:8 says, "Remember the Sabbath day, to keep it holy."

Zimbabwe brought me one other spiritually enlightening moment. I was wandering the city on a Sunday morning in search of a church to attend. I never found a church, but I got to know the city a bit better! That afternoon, I was crossing through a park to return back to where I was staying, and what I saw was amazing. As far as my eyes could see, there were people laying on the ground napping, relaxing, and taking care of one another.

At first, I couldn't even make sense of what I was seeing. Can you imagine seeing a large group of people basking in rest like that in the United States? They were not rushing to the next thing or looking to their calendars for the next appointment. They were taking in the day and resting. As a community, the Zimbabweans seem to have a literal understanding of Sabbath rest.

As part of the journey out of brokenness, it is important for both the pastor and the church to have time apart to pay attention to all of the steps required for God's healing to occur for everyone involved. I call this a "Healing Sabbath."

For the person dealing with brokenness, there has to be a time of ceasing from full-time ministry. Depending on the situation, a Healing Sabbath could mean more time away each week or it could mean a certain number of weeks away from the church. Whatever is appropriate for the situation, it is important to note that the church and the pastor need to come to a level of understanding, make a plan, and have an agreement on how to communicate the plan with the congregation.

The focus has to be on the components of the pastor's healing journey, and the only way to fully engage is to enter an extended time of healing rest. Please do not get this mixed up with a sabbatical. Sabbaticals are important and healthy, but this is not the time or the definition of a sabbatical.

A Healing Sabbath is all about creating the time and space to work on the areas of brokenness that have come to light and take steps toward possible restoration back into the ministry setting. It is completely realistic that a church might not know if the outcome of the process will lead to a return to ministry or not. There are too many complex scenarios for us to discuss here, and it is important to remember that anything is possible for our mighty God.

My Healing Sabbath did not come at the invitation of my current church, but rather after my decision to step down and leave the situation. I knew before I could move on to my next ministry setting, I had to work on some things and reflect on what had happened. I used this time to mourn the loss of my church and the wonderful people I had truly grown to love. I also needed time to accept the death of some dreams I had for the church and the surrounding community.

It is important for all of us to consider the time of rest God has called us to. Ezekiel 20:19-20 says, "I am the Lord your God; walk in my statutes, and be careful to obey my rules, and keep my Sabbaths holy that they may be a sign between me and you, that you may know that I am the Lord your God."

We are designed to spend time with God. In that time, we will find rest. A time of rest with God gives us a recognition of things like hope, encouragement, victory, peace, and healing.

Each day, we awaken with new mercy and new hope. We are refreshed by God to move into a new day. Each day, we also have moments that tear at the tapestry of the perspective and purpose God is weaving into our lives. God is available to us daily to heal and to give us rest. If we are not stepping into this precious opportunity, how can we expect to thrive?

I found help during my extended Healing Sabbath. More importantly, I now recognize that I need to accept God's loving and gracious invitation to *daily* Healing Sabbath found by being still in God's presence. This is a gift from God!

Reflection and prayerful self-examination led by the Holy Spirit are essential components of the healing process. Reflection helps us get after the "Why did I do that?" question. You have to be real when you reflect. Further reflection helps us answer the question, "What do I need to let go of?"

It is helpful not only to engage in private reflection, but also to seek out helpful and wise listeners. I am tremendously thankful that I was given the gift of time to do these things. My Healing Sabbath allowed me to seek out the people who could help me see what I was unable to see—especially those areas of wounding that had gone on for years without any processing. It gave me time to confirm and affirm what God has always thought of me, and to understand that my brokenness doesn't change His opinion of me.

God is good all the time, and all the time God is good. He is not just good when things are going well. He is the same yesterday as He is today and into the days ahead. He does not change, because I've changed nor does He turn His face when I fail. God stands ready to receive us right where we are. He promises that if we confess before Him, He will bring healing to us. That divine healing is good for our families, our communities, and our churches.

A Healing Sabbath grants time to cry out to God for help to focus on Him versus focusing on our pain or guilt. "When the righteous cry for help, the Lord hears and delivers them out of all their troubles" (Psalm 34:17). He strengthens our hearts and our minds as the Holy Spirit does the work of bringing us to a place of peace and comfort. This is not anything we can do for ourselves. We need divine intervention that can only come from God in His time.

Psalm 34:18 tells us, "The Lord is near to the brokenhearted and saves the crushed in spirit." This verse describes exactly what I was feeling and trying to fight through. What I needed most was a refuge, a place of care that would deal with my emotional wounds and spiritual needs. Are you in a position to do that for someone? Do you need to create a care team who will listen to your feelings and struggles and help you gain healing and restoration?

Psalm 34:22 says, "The Lord redeems the life of his servants; none of those who take refuge in him will be condemned." God provided a refuge in the people who picked up the assignment to care for me. Chances are, you have experienced or will someday experience this blessing in your life as well.

As God moved in me and His healing work was being seen by others, He invited me to pour into the life of someone else. It was clear God had plans to use these experiences to help others.

It was at this point of confirmation of how God planned to work in and through me that I heard the term, "wounded healer." Here I am with wounds exposed, and God asked me to pour out what had been poured into me. He was asking me to help bring someone else to a place of healing. I didn't necessarily feel ready, but this should not have been a surprise. God seems to do some of His best work in us when we don't feel completely qualified!

When you are feeling that you need to be served, find something or someone you can serve. It's counterintuitive, but it's exactly what you need to feed your soul. If God can use a wounded healer who is in the midst of healing, God can use anyone.

This is likely one of the biggest lessons the Church can learn. It has been said that a church should look more like an emergency room than a plush hotel. One of the great purposes of today's church is to be a place of healing, yet we aren't always equipped with a plan for how to walk alongside someone who needs help. It's messy. The world says to ditch them. Helping sometimes backfires. What would our churches and communities look like if we bravely faced our calling to be a place of healing for those who need it.

It's important to recognize that the brokenness of a pastor will have an impact on the church that must be addressed. I know that I deeply hurt people in my church. They weren't crazy or off base for feeling hurt. I disappointed them. I am very aware that I broke the trust that they placed in me. They wanted to gain insight into my experience with God through my sermons and many felt they were not able to do that. I had not shown my whole self to them through my preaching.

When there is brokenness or failure by a pastor, the congregation has an important role and opportunity. It is terribly difficult for a congregation with a flailing leader to come together with a unified response, but it is possible with good preparation and much prayer! Lay leaders are a crucial component and so is the creation of a defined process they will follow when the difficult circumstance comes. Congregations need to be willing to look closely at their motives, reactions, side conversations, and in general, the way they respond. We all need to be wary of hidden agendas and selfish ambitions during such stressful times.

Just like individuals, church congregations can carry baggage and unspoken, even unrecognized, woundedness that they carry for years, which God is anxious to work on. God loves an opportunity to work in the body of believers. Wounded congregations with unresolved conflicts and disappointments from the past *will* hurt people without anyone even realizing it. It can result in people fading into the background and eventually isolating themselves or leaving the faith community altogether.

*When there is brokenness
or failure by a pastor,
the congregation has an
important role and opportunity.
It is terribly difficult for
a congregation with a
flailing leader to come together
with a unified response,
but it is possible with
good preparation and
much prayer!*

I believe some congregations have become sanctuaries of shame and hiding. Sadly, in these churches, safety is only found when a person has an "acceptable failure." But if safety is only found in acceptable failure, is it really *safety* at all?! Congregations that are focused on prayer and God's word, with solid leadership across all pastors and staff, tend to have a much better, more unified response when adversity comes.

Because we know that when leadership changes, the definition of an acceptable failure can change overnight! I think this is one of many things people unconsciously fear whenever there is a change in the lead pastor or even chairman of the board. Fear can quickly take the form of critique.

A hurting, fearing congregation can act out of that pain in ways that seem uncharacteristic. Just like the hurting pastor, the congregation also needs to face its hurts and fears and seek God's healing! This is an incredibly hard journey, but with God, it is possible. Let us never forget that the Church, the larger Body of Christ, is called to be a refuge of healing for people, even for those in leadership.

Take some time to consider the following verses:

Exodus 15:26: "for I am the Lord, your healer."

Psalm 147:3: "He heals the brokenhearted and binds up their wounds."

Jeremiah 3:22: "'My wayward children,' says the LORD, 'come back to me, and I will heal your wayward hearts.'"

God our healer—Jehovah-Rapha—is the one who heals. God is more interested in us being holy than in being physically healthy and happy. Do not get me wrong. I like my physical health, and I like to be happy, but my body will one day be redeemed. God can bring about healing on this side of glory, but that will always be in His timing and in His will. Many people wonder why we do not see the power of God at work in us today, but I think we have a God who is doing His healing work today within us. God's great healing work is evident in each one of us, for His glory.

Many of us have spent far too many years in the shackles of unprocessed hurts, distorted messages, backward thinking about who we are, and the shameful actions we have taken. Is it possible that there has been little to no movement spiritually because we have yet to allow God to touch those areas? He is Jehovah-Rapha, the one who forgives all our iniquities, the one who heals all our diseases. Read Psalm 103:3 and be encouraged!

God wants each of us to live a life of peace. "Behold, I will bring to it health and healing, and I will heal them and reveal to them an abundance of prosperity (peace) and security" (Jeremiah 33:6). God is more than able to see deep within us and survey our hearts, cleansing us of bitterness, pride, and untruths along with any sin that may lead to afflictions of the heart.

Our God, the Great Physician, Jehovah-Rapha, is ready for you and me to turn to Him for the healing we have longed for or thought was impossible. The time is now! Forget about yesterday and do not wait for tomorrow.

REFLECTIONS ON THE JOURNEY

As a way to enter into a conversation with God about restoration, take some time to give thanks and rejoice in God's character and promise, turning to Him in faith and in love. Read the verse below and develop a Prayer, Petition, and Praise based on the chapter and verse.

Proverbs 4:20-22

"My son, be attentive to my words; incline your ear to my sayings. Let them not escape from your sight; keep them within your heart. For they are life to those who find them, and healing to all their flesh."

Prayer (confession and listening) _____

_____

_____

_____

Petition (our needs) _____

_____

_____

_____

Praise (bringing Him glory) _____

_____

_____

_____

CHAPTER ELEVEN

RADICAL FORGIVENESS

How do we know when to extend forgiveness? I'm talking about radical forgiveness that rises above how we feel, what we think should happen, our gut reactions, or our righteous justification. This makes me think of Jesus on the cross in Luke 23:34. Jesus forgave the criminals on His left and right while hanging on the cross. On this earth, we expect retaliation and retribution, but Jesus' way proves to be so very different. He pardoned the executioner. He forgave him in real-time. There was no waiting to see if the criminals would live out their lives differently. Jesus just forgave them.

You may be thinking: *Well, the criminals still died.* This is true, but I find that there is some healthy tension here for us to live into. We have an opportunity on this side of glory to demonstrate forgiveness in a way that the world rarely sees. Forgiving and continuing to do life with one in need of our forgiveness is both complex and rewarding.

Can a church in the right situation go beyond the sentiment of forgiveness to a place of action? Restoration takes action. It takes gutsy action. I am in no way suggesting that this is an easy thing to do, but on the other hand, as Christ-followers, when did we start to think that living out our discipleship would be easy?

Let's remember that our church is an assembly of people who have been impacted and transformed by the saving grace of Jesus Christ through His death and resurrection. We have recognized that we are sinners in need of a Savior. The Greek word that we translate as church is *ekklesia* and means "called out ones." [12] I would add that we are a reflection of the one who transformed us. The very nature of who we are to be as the Church is to go beyond the ordinary to the godly.

Every day, the called-out ones reflect and display the grace and mercy that have been poured on them. Every action, conversation, and situation can be an opportunity dripping with the grace they've been given. As the called-out ones, Christians should look and act differently than the world. Again, I know this is easier said than done because we are all sinful humans, but we must rise above the difficulty in order to display the restorative power of our God.

If a church body can continue to become deeply rooted in who it is called to be, then there is a solid chance that there is common ground to be found in a situation of brokenness. A church can forgive, restore, and receive a pastor back to the role of shepherd if it is done prayerfully with good leadership and a solid plan. A church with a vision for healing is a church that is ready to handle the toughest of situations.

It is true that people everywhere are dealing with some kind of brokenness. This is why we must see pastors like people who are just as much a part of the church as anyone else. We, the called-out ones, exist to glorify God. Read Ephesians 3:1-6, 12, 14 to ponder this further.

Preacher and author, John Piper, gives a powerful description of the role of the Church in his blog article called, "The Cosmic Church." Piper says, "Most of us go through day after day and seldom feel the impact of the magnitude of what we are caught up in by belonging to Jesus Christ.... And we don't take enough time to meditate on how our jobs, our home life, our leisure, our church involvement—how each of these fit into the cosmic significance of the church"[13]

We should consider that God may be using the church to bring about change in the people and in the pastor. Below are some questions for a church to consider on its journey to becoming a healing church for the brokenness of you, me, a pastor, or that person who wanders in because they just moved in across the street.

Let us not forget the grounding factor of who we are and who we are called to be. We are people filled with love which was first extended to us by the originator of that love.

Henri Nouwen says in his book, *Following Jesus*: "The original love is the original blessing. The original love is the original acceptance."[14] We should always strive to allow the love given to us to outweigh the circumstances of our current situations. It is God's love that allows us to love one another. Henri Nouwen goes on to say, "It is the first love that is the basis for all creative human relationship."

It is that first love that should guide and inform us when dealing with brokenness in our churches. It should look no different for people who fill the pews than it does for the one who fills the pulpit. We all have a faulty human condition in certain (or many) areas of our lives. We have wounds, possibly from our pasts, that are informing our present. Some can be seen, while others hide in the shadows.

The wound of rejection is one of the wounds that many of us deal with. As you know by now, this is true for me as well. This wound speaks to an experience of not being fully loved, says Nouwen. When I came to Christ nearly forty years ago, I believe I heard God say to me, "I love you no matter what, Terrance." At that time, I desperately needed to hear those words. It began a journey in figuring out that

I could trust that love in *all* areas of my life. God's love has moved me in powerful ways in many areas. Sometimes it comes slowly, and sometimes it comes quickly.

I share this with you because I believe with all my heart and soul that the Church must stand firm in this gift that has been given to the assembled people of God and demonstrate it to a world that says we should cancel or discard people when their brokenness starts to show. The assembled people of God are gathered to be light in the darkness and salt to preserve and cleanse.

How are we doing with being the salt and the light? How are we making disciples? How are we setting the stage for worship? How are we demonstrating grace and mercy to others?

We have to be willing to ask questions that will prepare the body of believers—the followers of Christ—to be a place of healing. Let us be so transformed by God's love that we can love people amid their brokenness.

When we come in touch with God's love, we are free to love people without asking for anything in return. Luke 6:34-35 tells us to love without expecting anything in return. I believe there is a space where churches can be about the work of forgiveness, reconciliation, restoration, and even reinstating a pastor, all in God's timing. It will take time, prayer, and hard work, but a church can arrive at a place where God's original love is the foundation for all decisions, big and small. It equips them to extend love in radical ways.

Now is the time to step forward into all that God asks of the Church. We need to take action in ways that shake our cultural status quo. Within our inherited position as daughters and sons of the living God, lies our power and responsibility as His Church. We are meant to be the head and not the tail. We are meant to display leadership to a world that desperately needs to be led. But what are we showing the world if we can't extend to others the very grace that has been extended to us? Again, I am under no illusion that this is easy. Just as I had to take a good look at what led me to use the words of others in my sermons without giving credit, Christians must take a good look at what is causing them to fall short of living out God's purpose and love. We are to reflect God's love poured out through the death and resurrection of our Lord and Savior, Jesus Christ.

What's our motivation to work toward being a healing church, the kind of church that lives out a call that honors God by displaying His glory? We do not have to look far for motivation. We only have to consider the words of Paul in Romans 1:1-5. Paul says that he is an apostle set apart for the Gospel. Like Paul, we have received grace and apostleship to bring about obedience through faith in God. We have been included in the same call as Paul, because we belong to Jesus Christ. There's our motivation.

We—the Church—are to extend grace to one another as God has extended grace to each of us. We all should attempt to be more like Paul who was eager to preach the Gospel. Let it be the same for the Church of Christ that we would be eager to extend grace. Sometimes, and understandably so, it is hard to forgive when we have been rocked by another person's actions. God's forgiveness is for all of us! Even amid our disobedience, God forgives us.

We do not have the fortitude to forgive in the manner God does, so it is on our knees that we must come before God, crying out as His set-apart ones, requesting His strength to forgive others. Left to our fleshly emotions, we will fall short every time. God has provided a way to extend supernatural power to forgive, and it is through Him that we can experience the divine architect of forgiveness. We all recognize that there are scenarios in which a pastor experiencing brokenness will need to leave his/her congregation, but that does not

Now is the time to step forward
into all that God asks of the Church.
We need to take action in ways
that shake our cultural status quo.
Within our inherited position as
daughters and sons of the living God,
lies our power and responsibility
as His Church. We are meant
to be the head and not the tail.
We are meant to display leadership
to a world that desperately needs
to be led. But what are we showing
the world if we can't extend to
others the very grace that has been
extended to us?

mean the church shouldn't be involved in God's great gift of healing and restoration.

Take some time to consider the following verse.

Hebrews 12:15 says, "See to it that no one fails to obtain the grace of God; that no 'root of bitterness' springs up and causes trouble, and by it many become defiled."

Forgiving can lead us to further disappointment and hurt if the sin happens again. Not forgiving can lead us to fall short of the grace-filled life God has for us. This can lead to a root of bitterness that affects the entire body. I would like us to consider that we best deal with bitterness head on. This is one benefit to keeping pastors attached to the church. It might be similar to a couple prematurely ending their relationship in divorce, citing their irreconcilable differences and the sheer work that it would take to get right with each other. Of course, there are "deal breakers" in a marriage, but just as a church is called to consider forgiving and helping a pastor through a period of brokenness, a husband and wife might be called to do the hard work of extending forgiveness to one another and letting God heal their marriage.

There are far too many churches going on about their daily business that have not dealt with their flaws or brokenness because they released the pastor and washed their hands of the situation. The church can be left with bitterness that is carried forward into the next person who will be their new shepherd. This may even have a legacy over two or three pastoral generations. Bitterness is the bait of Satan. The goal of the evil one is to bring us out of our senses to respond out of selfishness and bitterness.

Author, John Bevere, talks about the potential for bitterness in his book, *The Bait of Satan: Living Free from the Deadly Trap of Offense*. Bevere says if we are not careful, our hearts can harden, our eyes of understanding can dim, God's vision for grace can be distorted, and we might even withhold forgiveness.[15] I believe that you would agree with me when I say the Church of Jesus Christ is better than lingering roots of bitterness. Greater is He than the one who attempts to get footholds in our lives and in our churches.

There are far too many churches going on about their daily business that have not dealt with their flaws or brokenness because they released the pastor and washed their hands of the situation. The church can be left with bitterness that is carried forward into the next person who will be their new shepherd. This may even have a legacy over two or three pastoral generations. Bitterness is the bait of Satan. The goal of the evil one is to bring us out of our senses to respond out of selfishness and bitterness.

REFLECTIONS ON THE JOURNEY

As a way to enter into a conversation with God about restoration, take some time to give thanks and rejoice in God's character and promise, turning to Him in faith and in love. Read the verse below and develop a Prayer, Petition, and Praise based on the chapter and verse.

Ephesians 4:31-32

"Get rid of all bitterness, rage and anger, brawling and slander, along with every form of malice. Be kind and compassionate to one another, forgiving each other, just as in Christ God forgave you."

Prayer (confession and listening) _____

_____

_____

_____

Petition (our needs) _____

_____

_____

_____

Praise (bringing Him glory) _____

_____

_____

_____

CHAPTER TWELVE

PURSUIT OF GOD

As people who say we are born again and follow Him, pursuing God is our most important task. Before I go any further on this topic, please know that I am not suggesting we achieve or even portray perfection. Because you will have, just as I have, moments of falling short. This is not about how well we do or how often we get it done. It is, however, about coming to a better place of discovering or re-discovering that there is life to be experienced in spending time with God. This is something that we far too easily lose or forget in the hustle of life.

As you consider the process we have discussed, do so with the understanding that the foundation must be our pursuit of God. Any other foundation will not suffice. Consistent time with God will result in a deeper relationship with Him.

When I began my belief in Christ at age seventeen, I believed in the God who created the heavens and the earth. I believed in the God who called Abram and changed his name to Abraham. I was encouraged by the God who brought His people out of bondage. It moved my soul to know that God could take a shepherd boy and make him a king. I believed that "God so loved the world that He gave His only Son and whoever would believe would not perish but have everlasting life" (John 3:16).

During my Healing Sabbath, the time I spent in between churches, I was reminded of the greatest truth of all. I was grateful for this opportunity to be refreshed and to remember that in the course of doing ministry and life, it's easy to lose ourselves in whatever the current *things of life* may be.

It is critically important that we keep the real thing before us. The real thing I am talking about is Romans 8:38-39: "For I am sure that neither death nor life, nor angels nor rulers, nor things present nor things to come [I would add things in the past], nor powers, nor heights nor depth, nor anything else in all creation, will be able to separate us [me] from the love of God in Christ Jesus our Lord." I hope these verses speak to you as they spoke to me in a new and refreshing way.

Since I grew up in the foster care system with little to no contact with my biological parents, I desperately desired to be loved. I was suspicious of whether or not anyone loved me, but when I came into a relationship with Jesus Christ, I heard Him say, "I will love you forever!"

I counted on that love in my life from that moment forward. That love carried me through college when I thought college would be impossible for me. God's love raised me above the history of a broken family and raised me above the trauma caused by growing up with a lack of stable, loving relationships. His love raised me above my dyslexia. His love enabled me to find the love of a good woman and create a family grounded in stability, care, and service to one another, even though I did not have any examples upon which to draw from.

It was also God's love that allowed me to hear His call into pastoral ministry. It was God's love that I trusted when I heard Him say He wanted to use my life experiences to speak into the lives of others.

Somewhere along the way, the world clamored for my attention, and I let it become bigger and louder than God's voice. During my time of renewal, I was reminded that it is because of His love that I am called into action from this day forward. I try to respond to life out of my deep and abiding relationship with the One who first loved me, and I can love generously because of His love for me. I give what He has gifted me to give.

Too often, we work and see situations out of our human flesh. We try to look spiritual, but we don't give God the time of day. We need to stop allowing our day to own us. The day *is* God's! The world will distract and rob us of this joyful truth if we don't resist.

There is no perfection here, let me tell you. It's not uncommon for me to struggle to attend to my relationship with my Lord. There are days I have amazing victories, and there are days I have epic failures. It is the same yesterday, today, and for all the days ahead.

There are many promises we should hold onto. They are only for the taking if we are abiding in the vine of Christ. Listen to what John 15:5 has to say. (Be sure to check out verses 1-9 too.) "I am the vine; you are the branches. If you remain in me and I in you, you will bear much fruit; apart from me, you can do nothing." Our pursuit of God is about a connecting relationship with Christ who stands ready to abide in us in such a way that we bear fruit for the Kingdom of God.

What keeps us from abiding in God's love? There are many reasons. Some are valid, while others are just excuses. Whatever the reason(s), we have a God who has a deep desire to commune with us. I have experienced the words of Jeremiah 2:13: "For my people have committed two evils: they have forsaken me, the fountain of living waters, and hewed out cisterns for themselves, broken cisterns that can hold no water."

Do you find those words hard to hear? I know I did, I do, and I probably always will. These words are a mirror that we must look into. We have a God who pours out living water, and we become content with building vessels that we believe will satisfy the thirst within us. We have turned our backs on what God has provided and put self-reliance in the place where God should stand.

We, like those of Jeremiah's time, are being called to repentance. God has promised He will be merciful and filled with grace. God has given us a shepherd in Jesus Christ and empowerment through the Holy Spirit. This gift of renewal doesn't mean things will always be perfect. It is about moving from performing to enjoying and anticipating the growth that has been promised. It is during these times of renewal that God transforms and prepares me for the work He has called me to do.

Our relationship with God is not transactional, it is transformational! Transformation with God only comes from surrendering everything, not just the parts that are easy to surrender. On this side of glory, we work hard at performing in the right ways to gain the applause of people, thinking it will satisfy our need to be valued. All of us have core longings and needs that we seek to get filled by something or someone. Core longings are our deep, inward, desperate cries to find meaning and acceptance. We want love, security, understanding, purpose, significance, and a sense of belonging.

I know that because of some of the distortions in my life, growing up without parents and my learning disability, I felt it was natural that I would have some unmet needs. I learned, in fact, that God designed and gave me these needs and then graciously and fully supplied my every need! When I felt unloved, it was God who loved me all along. When I felt rejected, it was God who accepted me. When my core longings collided with my unprocessed pain, loss, and failure, I made decisions that were sinful and let other people down.

When we do not live on the living water that God provides, we run ourselves into a cycle of intense striving, falling short, and total failure. What keeps me from enjoying the living water of God the most is my need to attain the affirmation of people. How about you?

Seeking the approval of men is not what God has for us. After much self-reflection and studying of God's word, I can say that God is my total source. He is all that I am; all that I need is tied up in my abiding in Him. With God as my total source of worthiness, I do not have to perform, nor do I need the approval of people. In Christ, we are loved, and we are valued no matter what. I hope this brings you as much encouragement as it does me.

We are told in Romans 5:8, "But God shows His love for us in that while we were still sinners, Christ died for us." How extraordinary is that? God did not wait to show His love to us when we had it all worked out and pulled together; instead, it was right in the midst of our brokenness that He offered His great gift of grace.

That's just the starting place. Romans 5:10 says, "For if while we were enemies we were reconciled to God by the death of His Son, much more, now that we are reconciled, shall we be saved by his life." It is because of this incredible gift we can rejoice in the reconciliation that we have received, and we can extend reconciliation to others. We are recipients of reconciliation because of the work of Jesus Christ. Our call as Christ followers is to live out the ministry of reconciliation with one another. It is that call that should be seen operating within the body of believers and especially with those who take up the role of pastor.

Let's consider one aspect of pursuing God that has served me well over the years. Music has always been a great soother of my heart. When I made the decision to end my time at the church I was pastoring, I moved through the grief of losing access to the people I had grown to love. It was clear that I needed to find healing, and by now, you know a lot about the process I went through to find that healing. What I haven't shared is that I was greatly blessed by the power of music during my journey. As a matter of fact, the first thing I did was turn to music. I created a playlist that I called "Faith Builder." On this playlist, I included song titles like: "I Trust You" by James Fortune & FIYA, "Increase My Faith" by Brain Courtney Wilson, "I Need a Word" and "God is Able" by Smokie Norful, "Break Every Chain" by Tasha Cobbs Leonard, "Free Free" by BeBe Winans, and many others.[16] Music has a way of opening you up or preparing you for what God wants to say to you. My wise aunt said many important things that helped my spiritual growth. One of the greatest things she told me was, "Nephew, anything you want from God is tied up in the praise."

I learned that worship and praise are essential to my pursuit of God. So, I encourage you to find music that speaks to you. For me, urban contemporary and gospel choirs move my soul and deliver me to the throne room of God. You have to be willing to take the time to allow the lyrics and melody to penetrate to your core. You might feel this way about a different genre of music, but if you haven't witnessed the power of music and the act of praising God through music, explore that possibility this week. Music helps me rediscover my desperate need to make room for God. He is what I treasure most. Let's not leave our worship and praise only to Sunday morning.

Take some time to consider the following verse. 1 Chronicles 22:19: "Now set your mind and heart to seek the LORD your God. Arise and build the sanctuary of the LORD God, so that the ark of the covenant of the LORD and the holy vessels of God may be brought into a house built for the name of the LORD."

We cannot come to a place of any level of healing without running after God. This includes finding the truth of where we are in relationship with Him. Even though I came to Christ many years ago, there was a time in more recent years that I found myself feeling lost. I found my way back to enjoying the presence of our living God. In 1 Corinthians 6:19, it says, "Or do you not know that your body is a temple of the Holy Spirit within you, whom you have from God? You are not your own."

We are the temple of the Holy Spirit, and we must attend to the temple. In my pursuit of God, I was touched in places that I never considered needed healing. Never again would I want to go through that depth of despair, but at the same time, I am thankful for the experience because I now have new depth in my relationship with my King.

REFLECTIONS ON THE JOURNEY

As a way to enter into a conversation with God about restoration, take some time to give thanks and rejoice in God's character and promise, turning to Him in faith and in love. Read the verse below and develop a Prayer, Petition, and Praise based on the chapter and verse.

Zechariah 8:21

"The inhabitants of one city shall go to another, saying, 'Let us go at once to entreat the favor of the Lord and to seek the Lord of hosts; I myself am going."

Prayer (confession and listening) _____

_____

_____

_____

Petition (our needs) _____

_____

_____

_____

Praise (bringing Him glory) _____

_____

_____

_____

CHAPTER THIRTEEN

LIVING IN FREEDOM

My life and ministry verse has always been 2 Corinthians 3:17: "Now the Lord is Spirit, and where the Spirit of the Lord is, there is freedom." Some translations use "liberty" in place of "freedom." I like the word liberty. I realize this may just be semantics, but freedom seems like something granted to us because of who we are, while liberty seems like something undeserved that we are brought into.

Through my Healing Sabbath, I was liberated from bondage. It was nothing my church did to me. It was so much deeper. It was the bondage of my life experience of being rejected, alone, broken, unusable, and just not enough to be of any good. This brokenness had an impact on my quality of life, and I had never faced it or realized it.

As Christians, we have *Good News*. The God of Abraham, Isaac, and Jacob has given us promises to light our way to the truth of who we are. He handcrafted us after all. Ephesians 2:10 says, "For we are His workmanship (handiwork), created in Christ Jesus for good works, which God prepared beforehand, that we should walk in them."

All of who God created us to be has been considered, calculated, strategically designed, and birthed for His glory. All we have to do is walk into the divine handiwork. This may not be true for you, but it certainly has been true for me. There are parts of me that I continue to see as broken. I know I shouldn't, but I can't completely shake the mindset or erase the doubt. God knew and planned for every part of who I would be. Even my dyslexia has and will be used for His good work. I have lived most of my life working out of my perceived deficit. All along, God has used it to teach me empathy for people who have a learning disability or another reason for the world perceiving them as not enough. We must learn to see ourselves as God sees us. We are loved by God in a way that cannot be contained. "In this is love, not that we have loved God but that He loved us and sent His Son to be the propitiation for our sin" (1 John 4:10).

God has created us out of that love. We are exactly what He had in mind! We are even designed for specific work that He has in mind for us. God knows us, and we are not alone. "Consider the ravens: they neither sow nor reap, they have neither storehouse nor barn, and yet God feeds them. Of how much more value are you than the birds" (Luke 12:24).

Let me tell on myself for a moment. I have spent a good portion of my ministry life trying to live up to what others thought I should be. I have allowed their evaluation of me to feed me. Boy, did I get that twisted! God is the only one I can derive my value from. God is the only one who I can allow to feed me each day.

How about you? How have you allowed this world to feed you? Be done with all of that and allow God to liberate you into the promises set before you!

Years ago, when I was a church planter, we prayerfully considered what the name of the church might be. We landed on The Compass. I wanted people to know that there is only one way to set the course of their lives. We have a purpose in this life, and the remainder of my ministry is dedicated to helping people not only see God's purpose but also to live it.

Ephesians 3:17-19 says, "So that Christ may dwell in your hearts through faith that you, being rooted and grounded in love, may have the strength to comprehend with all the saints what is the breadth and length and height and depth, and to know the love of Christ that surpasses knowledge, that you may be filled with all the fullness of God."

If we want to know the fullness of God and His love for us in every area, then we need to bathe every area of our lives in this truth, particularly the ones we tend to try to hide. We may not all have the same purpose in God's Kingdom, but we all do have a Kingdom purpose. It's important as believers that we help one another discover our Kingdom purpose.

One of the things that my wife, Michelle, and I agreed upon in raising our children was to give them a sense of purpose. We have adopted the family motto: "The Rollerson Family Serves." We wanted our kids to know that they do not live at the center of the universe, and their overarching purpose is to serve others. Truth be told, our family motto did not always go over well! But by the grace of God, our children have "service to others" at their core, and we have been blessed to see it play out in different ways in their adult lives. We are called by God to love our neighbors as ourselves, and sometimes that may even come at a cost. It's a cost I am happy to pay because it sets my heart right before our holy God.

As a kid growing up in the foster care system, I spent some of my days wondering where I belonged and who I belonged to. When I turned fourteen, I was given the opportunity to meet and eventually live with my biological family. Learning about who my people were brought a level of fulfillment. I am thankful for my biological family because their love for me was there even when I did not know them. It is a precious thing to belong. Belonging stabilizes our foundation.

Over the years, I have gained great insight into my extended family on both my mother's side and absent father's side. I have learned about the power of family as well as the consequences of brokenness in a family. All of it has played into my life experience, but it is the power of belonging to God's family that has truly stabilized me. Ephesians 2:6-7 says, "And God raised us up with him and seated us with him in the heavenly places in Christ Jesus, so that in the coming ages he might show the immeasurable riches of his grace in kindness toward us in Christ Jesus. There is no better place to belong than in the grace of God."

Ephesians 1:11-12 adds, "In him we have obtained an inheritance, having been predestined according to the purpose of him who works all things according to the counsel of his will, so that we who were the first to hope in Christ might be to the praise of his glory."

We live in a world and culture that at the least, distorts and at the most, blinds us from the reality of who we were created to be. I choose God to set my value, to model the pattern of love, to chart the course of my life, and to liberate me from all my shackles, including the shackles that are fur-lined and so comfortable I choose to continue to wear them! I say to all those who may be reading these words: Who the Lord sets free is free indeed. On this day, claim your liberation!

Is there a biblical guideline for how and why a church can and should make the effort to work with a pastor who finds himself or herself with an area of brokenness? I have yet to find a place in the Bible that says we should not include our pastor as a member of our faith community, showing mercy and love when trouble comes.

It will not be easy. Liberation always comes at a cost. Some will think it to be too high a price to pay. Others will just not want to put in the effort. Take some time to consider the following verses in 2 Corinthians 3:17-18: "Now the Lord is the Spirit, and where the Spirit of the Lord is, there is freedom. And we all, with unveiled face, beholding the glory of the Lord, are being transformed into the same image from one degree of glory to another. For this comes from the Lord who is the Spirit."

I understand this text is talking about freedom from sin and death, but I would like us also to consider the things that are bringing us toward a slow death every day. It's the sin in our lives that is keeping us from healing from our past brokenness. We need to be set free.

It is such an amazing thing that we have a God who stands ready to meet us in our mess and deliver us into the freedom of His presence. Our surrendering to the work of transformation is a continuous process.

I would have hoped to come to grips with the issues of my younger life a little sooner so those issues could be in the ground and buried, but that has not been the case. God had a long and transformative work to do in my life, and I know he is not finished yet!

It's never too late. God is always ready to help us deal with issues long overdue. While I would have never volunteered to walk through the pain of my brokenness, I am thankful for the surfacing of issues and the timing of the spotlight as well. Issues left to their own devices will always choose to run and hide, but God wants them out in the open to remove the power they hold over us.

REFLECTIONS ON THE JOURNEY

As a way to enter into a conversation with God about restoration, take some time to give thanks and rejoice in God's character and promise, turning to Him in faith and in love. Read the verse below and develop a Prayer, Petition, and Praise based on the chapter and verse.

Galatians 5:1

"For freedom Christ has set us free; stand firm therefore, and do not submit again to a yoke of slavery."

Prayer (confession and listening) _____

_____

_____

_____

Petition (our needs) _____

_____

_____

_____

Praise (bringing Him glory) _____

_____

_____

_____

CHAPTER FOURTEEN

A BLESSING & A PRAYER

Let's start with the blessing. If you are a pastor or church leader and have found yourself in a place of brokenness, I pray God's blessing of Goshen (God's protection) for you. When we find ourselves feeling broken, the evil one tries to kick us while we are down.

This may come in all sorts of forms, including what we perceive people may be saying about us or what we may be thinking about ourselves. We need a refuge where we can stay, particularly during times of spiritual, emotional, and mental stress, to find safety, encouragement, hope, and truth.

Goshen was God's protected place for the Hebrew people. "Only in the land of Goshen, where the children of Israel were, was there no hail" (Exodus 9:26). God has a people, and He has a protected place for His people. In this place, there was no hail, no lightning, and no thunder. When there is madness all around us, I believe there is a place to rest in the tender care of God. Yes, our reality is that circumstances and situations will always be with us, but we do not have to be alone when dealing with them. We are always loved by

God. Amid disaster, God is still good, and God is still working it out for our good and for His glory.

In George Kirkpatrick's article called, "Goshen—God's Protected Place," he says, "As the Hebrew people were bearing witness the bottomless pit was opening, smoke was rising out of the pit, and out of the smoke came locusts. These locusts would destroy everything left by the hail. These were not only destroying locusts, these were stinging locusts. Their sting was like the sting of a scorpion. These stinging locusts would torment men for five months. They would make men's lives so miserable they would want to die, but death will flee from them." [17]

In Goshen, God's protected place for His people, God was seeing the clear light in the storm. The light, meaning understanding and knowledge, means God can see a clear path forward. Even in Goshen, which was controlled Egyptian land, the Lord brought prosperity to the children of Israel, and they grew their number.

Our God has the understanding and knowledge to deal with the storms in our lives. I do not know what your storm may be, but I have experienced mine. I have found my Goshen. I have found the place of truly understanding I am loved by God and nothing can or will separate me from the love of God. I do not expect that I have experienced my last storm, and you will have other storms come your way too. What I wholeheartedly want for you is to rest in God's protected place. My Goshen allowed me to rediscover God's deep love for me. The locusts had eaten some things in my life. I lost some opportunities. I felt pain. All the while, God's love remained the same, consistent and true.

Goshen can not only be a place of protection, but it can also be a place of preparation. As I write these words, God is preparing me. I do not know exactly what is before me, but I do know that I needed this time to be protected and to prepare. I pray God would bless you with the discovery of your Goshen as well.

It is my hope as you journey toward healing that a place of protection would be found for you. This life that we are living can be hard and seemingly unforgiving. We have a mighty God, and He is a refuge for each of us at our time of need.

If you were to read the book of Nahum, you would notice the theme of disaster. But with God, there is a safe place for those who choose Him. God's compassion and goodness are still available for the taking as you continue your journey of restoration. May it be a new place of deep abiding in the only one who can provide and protect.

When we fully and truly know that we have a place of provision with God, we can be set free from the things in our past and present that have held us toiling in bondage. My deepest desire is that each of you would know the same freedom given to me through the death and resurrection of Jesus Christ. It is ours by God's grace for the taking. *Find your Goshen!*

Churches, pastors, and everyday people who are willing to step into the journey of restoration during a time of brokenness, I'm praying for you. May God bless you on this journey as it will require strength and wisdom you did not even know you had. It will require a lot of self-reflection and an open mind.

There's something that I have noticed about how the grace of God works both in the Old Testament and in the New Testament. God does not go with the flow. He seems to move in radical ways that transform and disrupt the status quo. The Israelites expected rescue from Pharaoh, but they got the great I AM. They got the living God who wanted not only to free them from the physical bondage of slavery, but also to free them from the deeper things like fear and lack of trust in Yahweh. These things were keeping them enslaved even when they had been physically set free. He wants to free us too.

We stroll through life not fully realizing the power that we have extended to us through the death and resurrection of Jesus Christ. There is much freedom to be claimed if we would only allow God into the deepest, most hidden recesses of our soul. Like Adam in the garden, God knows where we are and is waiting for us to answer.

I pray that you can enter into the radical work of God's amazing grace and mercy. I pray that each of you can find rest, restoration, and renewal. May the Lord bless you and keep you. May He make His face shine upon you, strengthening you, and giving you peace. (Full prayer of blessing found in Numbers 6:24-26.)

May the God of all grace strengthen you and make you perfect before Himself. May He settle you in such a way that His peace rolls from your brow like a cool mountain stream. May God's grace-filled power move in and through you individually and corporately, even in times of disappointment and brokenness. With every word you speak, every action you take, and every thought you have, may you bring glory to the one who has found, claimed, saved, renewed, and restored us all.

Churches, pastors, and everyday people who are willing to step into the journey of restoration during a time of brokenness, I'm praying for you. May God bless you on this journey as it will require strength and wisdom you did not even know you had. It will require a lot of self-reflection and an open mind.

ABOUT THE AUTHOR

Terrance celebrates forty-one years of following Christ as his Lord, thirty years of marriage to Michelle, and twenty-two years of being ordained as a pastor. In his ministry, Terrance has enjoyed preaching the Word, counseling people of all ages, growing multi-ethnic/multi-cultural churches, and serving people in the community that are living in the margins. He earned a bachelor's degree from Bethel University in St. Paul Minnesota and a master's in divinity degree from Luther Seminary in St. Paul Minnesota. He is ordained with the Evangelical Covenant Church. Terrance holds several certifications in pastoral counseling, life coaching, and cultural intelligence, and is a facilitator of Fuller Seminary Micah Groups.

Terrance lives in Roseville, Minnesota, and enjoys time with family, cooking, cycling, participating in and watching sports, and seeing movies.

Terrance's hope and prayer is that God uses *Broken Yet Called* to bless the lives of people that have and will experience brokenness, and that churches would rise to the challenge of serving as a place of renewal and restoration.

You can find Terrance on Facebook as
The Urban Shepherd (facebook.com/urbanshepherd4u)
and Instagram @terrancerollerson

ENDNOTES

INVITATION

1. Newton, John, "Amazing Grace," https://www.hymnlyrics.org/mostpop-ularhymns/amazinggrace.php, access date, September 7, 2021.

2. Merriam-Webster, "Grace," https://www.merriam-webster.com/dictionary/grace, access date, November 5, 2021.

3. Tozer, Aiden Wilson, *The Knowledge of the Holy*, (HarperCollins: New York City, 1961).

4. MacArthur, John, *The Truth About Grace*, (Thomas Nelson:Nashville, 2012).

CHAPTER SIX

5. Rinck, Margaret Josephson, "Becoming a Healing Community," *Christianity Today*, published in 1992 article, republished in August 2000.

CHAPTER SEVEN

6. Owens, Nellie, "4 Things Everyone Should Know About Humility," https://activechristianity.org/4-things-everyone-should-know-about-humility, access date September 15, 2021.

7. Tatham, Colton, "Four Marks That Define Humbleness," https://unlock-ingthebible.org/2014/03/four-marks-that-define-humbleness/, March 31, 2014, access date September 5, 2021.

8. Warren, Rick, *The Purpose Driven Life: What on Earth am I Here for?* (Zondervan: Grand Rapids, 2002).

9. MacDonald, James, "The Altitude for Living," https://jamesmacdonaldmin-istries.org/the-altitude-for-living/, October 29, 2020, access date November 17, 2021.

CHAPTER NINE

10. Ogne, Steve and Roehl, Tim. *TransforMissional Coaching: Empowering Leaders in a Changing Ministry World*, (B&H Publishing: Nashville, 2008).

11. Maxwell, Victoria, "The 6 Steps of Healing You Need to Know," www.psychologytoday.com, April 21, 2015, access date September 8, 2021.

CHAPTER ELEVEN

12. Manser, Martin H. Zondervan Dictionary of Bible Themes, (Zondervan Publishing: Grand Rapids,1999).

13. Piper, John, "The Cosmic Church," www.desiringgod.org, March 21, 1981, access date September 11, 2021.

14. Nouwen, Henri, *Following Jesus: Finding Our Way Home in an Age of Anxiety*, Convergent Books: Colorado Springs, 2019.

15. Bevere, John, *The Bait of Satan: Living Free from the Deadly Trap of Offense*, (Charisma House: Lake Mary, Florida, 1994).

CHAPTER TWELVE

16. "I Trust You" by James Fortune & FIYA, Black Smoke Records, 2018, "Increase My Faith" by Brain Courtney Wilson, Motown Gospel Records, 2018, "I Need a Word" by Smokie Norful, Motown Gospel Records, 2014, "God is Able" by Smokie Norful, EMI Gospel Records, 2005, "Break Every Chain" by Tasha Cobbs Leonard, Motown Gospel Records, 2013, "Free Free" by BeBe Winans, Regimen Records, 2019.

CHAPTER FOURTEEN

17. Kirkpatrick, George, "Goshen—God's Protected Place," www.newfoundationspubl.org/goshen.htm, access date September 17, 2021.